You Can TRUST Your Bible

The Church of Christ
Tuscumbia, Alabama

You Can TRUST Your Bible

Lectures Delivered at the
University Christian Student Center
Oxford, Mississippi
January 23-24, 1976

Neale Pryor

QUALITY PUBLICATIONS

P.O. BOX 1060   ABILENE, TEXAS 79604

© Neale Pryor 1980

ISBN 0-89137-524-4

Table of Contents

DEDICATION

To my mother and father,
Mr. and Mrs. Neale B. Pryor,
who first taught me the Bible
and showed by their lives how
it should be lived.

Table of Contents

DEDICATION

To my mother and father,
Mr. and Mrs. Neale B. Pryor,
who first taught me the Bible
and showed by their lives how
it should be lived.

Introduction

"If I can't trust my Bible, what can I trust?" These were the words of a distraught woman after it was pointed out in a Bible class that a certain verse in her version gave the incorrect sense.

With the multiplication of English translations and the discovery of additional ancient materials, this fear has been voiced by many lovers of the Bible. Can I really trust my Bible? How can I know that I have the very words that God intended me to have?

There are four questions you must answer before deciding whether or not you can trust your Bible.

1. Is the Bible inspired? Is it the word of God or of man?

2. Are we sure that we have the right books in the Bible?

3. Can we be certain that we have the exact words of the writers?

4. How can we know if our Bible has been properly translated? If I don't know Hebrew or Greek, how can I really know what is being said?

These four questions will be answered in this work. There are good reasons for trusting our Bible. The fears of many regarding this matter are unfounded. May this work help the reader have a more certain faith in the reliability of the Scriptures and a greater appreciation of the Bible.

CHAPTER I
Is the Bible Inspired?

If you saw a rock hitting a can and you could not see where the rock was coming from, and then, another and another rock hit the can, before long you would conclude that someone was throwing at the can.[1] This is Richard Whately's way of illustrating the force of circumstantial evidence. This is the type of evidence that we have regarding the inspiration of the Bible. There are many threads of evidence, each one pointing to the same conclusion: the Bible is the inspired Word of God. Notice some of these arguments, all of these rocks that hit the can.

THE BIBLE CLAIMS TO BE INSPIRED

The Bible claims inspiration for itself. Of course, uninspired books could make the same claim. That fact alone does not make it inspired. But if a book were inspired, would it not make that claim? It would be strange if an inspired book never made any reference to its inspiration.

"For no prophecy was ever made by an act of human will, but men moved by the Holy Spirit spoke from God" (2 Peter 1:21).[2] These are the words of Peter regarding the Old Testament prophets. The word *moved* has the idea of being carried or borne along.

Holy men of old were carried along by the Holy Spirit. When they spoke, they were aware that their message was not their own, but God's.

"All Scripture is inspired by God and profitable for teaching, for reproof, for correction, for training in righteousness; that the man of God may be adequate, equipped for every good work" (2 Timothy 3:16, 17). Paul is here referring to the Old Testament scriptures; notice his reference to the fact that Timothy had known the Scriptures from a babe (v. 15). His Jewish mother had taught the Scriptures to him. But Paul is including more than just the Scriptures that Timothy had known from a babe. "All Scripture is inspired. . . ." Any writing that deserves the designation of *Scripture* is inspired. The word for *inspired* in 2 Timothy 3:16 means "God-breathed." The holy men who wrote the Scriptures had these words breathed into them by God.

When Jesus was talking to the apostles before sending them out on the limited commission, he warned them of the hardships that they would face. They would be arrested and would appear before governors and kings. But they were not to worry about how or what they would speak, "for it shall be given you in that hour what you are to speak. For it is not you who speak, but *it is* the Spirit of your Father who speaks in you" (Matthew 10:19, 20).

Jesus gave the apostles a similar promise of the Holy Spirit in his farewell discourse in John 14:26. "But the Helper, the Holy Spirit, whom the Father will send in My name, He will teach you all things, and bring to your remembrance all that I said to you." The word translated *helper* is literally *paraclete*. It means a friend who is called to the side of one in need.

When the apostles spoke by the Holy Spirit, their message was inspired. Would it not follow that when they wrote, the message was likewise inspired?

1 Corinthians 2:11-13 is one of the better scriptures on the claim of the Bible to be inspired.

> For who among men knows the thoughts of a man except the spirit of the man, which is in him? Even so the thoughts of God no one knows except the Spirit of God. Now we have received, not the spirit of the world, but the Spirit who is from God, that we might know the things freely given to us by God, which things we also speak, not in words taught by human wisdom, but in those taught by the Spirit, combining spiritual *thoughts* with spiritual *words*.

The first point is that only the spirit of a man knows what a man is thinking. Is it not wonderful that people cannot read the minds of others? Only a man's spirit knows his thoughts. Similarly, only the spirit of God knows the thoughts of God. That Spirit of God is the Holy Spirit.

The second point is that the apostles have received the Spirit from God. Consequently, they can know the thoughts of God.

The third point is that the thoughts of God have been put down in words which that Spirit taught the inspired men.

This passage is an excellent statement of verbal inspiration. The idea that the Spirit gave the general thought to the writers and let them put it down in their own words is not found here. The very words are inspired.

Galatians 3:16 has been used to teach verbal inspiration since Paul is there making an argument from the fact that the word *seed* is singular instead of plural. However, this is not a valid argument. The Hebrew word *seed (zera')* is a collective noun. It may be either singular or plural. Paul is giving an interpretation of the word, not making an argument from the number of the word.

There is much said about the different theories of inspiration. One preacher said, "I have no theory of inspiration; the Bible does not have a theory, so why should I?" It is true that the Bible does not give a theory of inspiration. There have been many theories suggested: plenary inspiration, thought inspiration, dictation theory—or even the flute theory!

The dictation theory would leave the impression that one day God said to Paul, "All right, Paul, get your pen out; today we are going to write 1 Corinthians. Start off now: 'The apostle Paul . . .' " Paul writes. "To the church of God." "At Corinth." "How do you spell Corinth, Lord?" "C-o-r-i-n-t-h." Surely, this was not the way the Bible was written.

One marvelous feature about inspiration of the Bible is that even though the different writers of the Bible were inspired by the same Spirit, they maintained their own distinctive styles. For example, one can read Luke and Acts in the Greek and easily tell that the style is completely different from that of Mark, or Matthew, or John or Paul. In fact, different levels of ability can be seen in the writing. Luke would probably get a grade of A; he is one of the best. Paul would get a B + . Some say that Hebrews could not have been written by Paul because it is in too polished a style for Paul. James is good; 1 Peter is good; but 2 Peter is not all that good. The epistles of John are in good style, but Revelation seems to have some grammatical errors in it.

These different men wrote as they knew how; they used words that they knew; and they used manners of expressions that were common to them. The spirit of God guarded those writers from error and yet conveyed the message through men and their own distinct personalities.

Another approach to a theory of inspiration could be called the flute theory. This is the theory that each writer says the same truth but through the medium of his personality it sounds different from that of another writer. Yankee Doodle played on a piano sounds different from the same tune played on a flute. So, when one writer tells the gospel story, he sounds one way, and another writer sounds another, but they both are playing the same tune, without any errors, without missing any notes.

Thought inspiration is the theory that the ideas and not the words are inspired. This is a safeguard against having to deal with any apparent contradictions, inaccuracies, doubtful textual readings and such like. This theory admits errors in the text. Yet the thought is still there. But this theory has its problems. If there are errors in some of the details, how can one be sure that there are not also errors in some of the teachings? Who can discern what may be errors and what are not?

The writers of the Bible maintained their distinctive personalities, and through their own personal styles of writing taught the eternal message, yet they were guarded from error. The combination of the human and divine is similar to the incarnation. Jesus of Nazareth was totally human, yet He was perfectly divine. The infallible message of God has been communicated through fallible men, in the language of man, in the distinctive styles of men; yet the book is more than the work of a man.

The books of the Bible were written for certain needs of the moment. It is doubtful that the Lord told Paul that the Christians needed another book to go into their Bible, so he was to write 2 Corinthians. Paul wrote this letter, and all of his letters, to deal with a specific need in the church at that time. Probably at the time of writing, Paul did not even realize that he was contributing another book to a collection later known as the New Testament.

There are three basic approaches to the authority of the Scriptures. The first is the old liberal view. This is the willingness to accept only what can be explained by human reason. Those who subscribe to this type of thinking refuse to accept the miraculous element in the Bible. The virgin birth, the physical resurrection of Jesus, and other miracles must be explained naturally or rejected. It makes one's reason the authority.

A more modern approach is the neo-orthodox or existential type of thinking. This is the willingness to accept as authority only what appeals to the individual's feelings. Advocates of this approach claim that the Bible is not the word of God; it *contains* the word of God. "What speaks to me" is the Word of God. What may be inspired to one person may not be inspired to another, because it does not "speak to him." From this type of thinking comes the adage, "Do your own thing." No one is to tell any other what he should or should not do. There are no absolutes in life; all is relative. The new morality is an outgrowth of this type of thinking.

The third view is the conservative orthodox view. The Bible definitely gives the impression that it considers itself to be the final authority and is to be taken literally. If one accepts the Bible, he must accept it on its own claim to be the final authority in matters of life and religion. Jesus himself said, "The scripture cannot be broken" (John 10:35). The Bible claims to be the inspired Word of God.

That is one rock that hits the can.

THE HISTORY OF THE BIBLE

The second rock that hits the can is the remarkable history of the Bible. There is no other book that more people have tried to destory than this one. And at the same time, there is today no more popular book than the Bible. Anything that can endure and outlive all the attacks upon it such as the Bible has experienced must be more than the work of a man.

"For you have been born again not of seed which is perishable but imperishable, *that is,* through the living and abiding word of God" (1 Peter 1:23). The Word of God is the seed of the kingdom (Luke 8:11). As long as the seed of the kindgom remains, the kingdom will remain. One may drive through Mississippi at a certain time of the year when there is no cotton in the fields and say, "There's no cotton in Mississippi any more." But wait until next spring, and he will see plenty of cotton in Mississippi. The farmers have saved the seed. When that seed is planted under the right conditions, the cotton will grow again.

There may be a period in the history of the church when one cannot find New Testament Christians or New Testament churches. But when that seed is planted in good and honest hearts, again there will be New Testament churches and Christians. The church is never dead as long as the seed is alive. That seed is the Word of God.

There have been at least three concentrated efforts to destroy the Bible or to curtail its influence. *The first of these* was by the Roman government. When the

Roman state persecuted Christians, they knew they would have to destroy their Word if they would ever destroy the church. In the days of Decius (249-251) and Diocletian (284-305), it was a capital offense to be found in possession of the Christian scriptures. That is probably why there are not many large manuscripts of the Scriptures before the fourth century. The only ones that were kept were those small enough to be hidden from the authorities.

Yet, shortly after these persecutions, Constantine commissioned Eusebius of Caesarea to produce some copies of the Christian scriptures. From the catacombs, closets, caves, etc., came the Christians with copies of their precious Word. It is possible that two of these copies exist today in the Codex Sinaiticus and the Codex Vaticanus. Rome is gone; the church is still here. The emperors are dead; the Word they sought to destroy lives on.

The second attack on the Bible is not one to destroy it so much as to limit its influence among the masses. The medieval church felt that the Bible should not be put into the hands of the masses because they were not skilled enough to deal with it. A child should not be given a loaded gun or sharp knife. Just so, the ignorant masses could not be entrusted to read and understand properly the Bible. The Bibles were chained to the pulpit in those days in order to keep people from stealing them, not to keep priests or others from reading them. The copies of the Bible were few and very expensive, since they were made by hand. Often a church would possess only one copy of the Scriptures, and even then perhaps not have the whole Bible.

The early English translators of the Bible met with stiff resistance. The first man to translate the Bible into English was John Wycliffe, in 1382. In 1428 at the

16

Council of Constance, some 44 years after his death, it was decreed that Wycliffe's bones should be dug up, that his body should be burned, and his ashes thrown into the river. Thomas Fuller commented on this: "They threw the ashes into the Swift. The Swift conveyed them into the Avon, the Avon into the Severn, the Severn into the narrow seas, they into the main ocean; and thus the ashes of Wycliffe are the emblem of his doctrine, which is now dispersed all the world over."[3]

The first man to print the New Testament into English was William Tyndale. He is called the Father of the English Bible. Tyndale had to print his Bible on the European continent and smuggle the Bibles back to England. He was finally apprehended and executed. The story is told that at his death Tyndale cried, "Lord, open the King of England's eyes!"[4] This prayer must have been answered in the next century. Later Bibles were produced with the approval of the English crown (Cloverdale's, the Great Bible, the Bishops' Bible, and, of course, the King James Version of 1611).

The third attack against the Bible is the skepticism of the modernist. Voltaire was one of the leaders of this movement in the 18th century. He boasted that it took 12 ignorant fishermen to establish Christianity, and he would show how one Frenchman could destory it. One ironic quirk of fate is that 25 years after Voltaire died, his home was purchased by the Geneva Bible Society and became a storehouse for the distribution of Bibles.[5]

After all of these attacks, and the continuing ones against the Bible even today, the Bible is the perennial best seller in the free world. It has been translated into more languages than any other. It is the best preserved book of antiquity. While other works by men who lived near the New Testament times have only one to 100 manuscripts extant, there are about 5,357 Greek

17

manuscripts of the New Testament. Add to that the Syriac, Latin and Coptic manuscripts, and the number is well over 10,000.

> Last eve I passed the blacksmith's door
> > And heard the anvil ring the vesper chime;
> When looking in, I saw upon the floor,
> > Old hammers worn with beating years of time.
>
> "How many anvils have you had," said I,
> > "To wear and batter all these hammers so?"
> "Just one," said he; then said with twinkling eye,
> > "The anvil wears the hammers out, you know."
>
> And so, I thought, the anvil of God's Word
> > For ages skeptics' blows have beat upon;
> Yet, though the noise of falling blows was heard,
> > The anvil is unharmed—the hammer's gone![6]

THE UNIQUENESS OF THE BIBLE

The third rock that hits the can is the uniqueness of the Bible. The Bible is in a class by itself. If there is a book that is divine, the Bible must be it. That which is second best is so inferior to it that it does not even compare.

Before one turns his back on the Bible, he had better ask where he is going to look. He should not give up something unless he has something better to turn to. When many of the Jews turned their backs on Jesus to walk no more with Him, Jesus turned to the 12 and asked them, "Will you also go away?" Perhaps Peter thought of leaving for the moment; then he considered where he might turn back to. There was no other place to turn. Peter replied, "To whom shall we go? You have the words of eternal life" (John 6:68).

If one discards the Bible, where will he turn? Consider the alternatives. Should he accept the writings of the Koran? What about the Hindu scriptures? The sayings of Buddha or Confucius? Or perhaps Ann Landers? These works are far inferior to the Bible. The Bible is unique—in a class by itself.

George Ernest Wright, a late professor of Harvard, wrote:

> Thousands of documents of every sort have been unearthed which can be compared with biblical literature and which help us greatly in understanding it. Yet amid the glorious ruins of Egypt, Syria, and Mesopotamia one still must stand amazed at the literary, poetic, and religious genius of Israel. The other nations had nothing which can be placed on the same level with the Bible.

These are the words of a man who has had opportunity to investigate writings of the ancients that the ordinary man will probably never see.

Where would anyone find a book with *teachings* that surpass those of the Bible? Where could the equal to the Golden Rule or the Sermon on the Mount ever be found?

What book portrays greater *literary genius* than does the Bible? Shakespeare cannot equal the literature of the Bible. Take for an example the book of Job, or the 23rd Psalm, or the Beatitudes. Where could a more majestic piece of writing be found than in the story of Creation in Genesis 1?

The *unity* of the Bible is amazing. The Bible was written over a period of about 1400 years by more than 40 authors; the names of some are not known. And yet, it is really not 66 books, but one book. It is THE BOOK, the Bible. The golden thread of redemption runs from Genesis to Revelation. It has to be the work of one mind—the mind of God.

The Bible is unique in its resourcefulness. The Bible is like a great piece of music. A beautiful symphony becomes even more beautiful as one hears it again and again. The listener can see beauty and harmony in the composition that escaped him the first time he heard it. The same is true with the Bible. No one can say, "I read the Bible once. Now I am through with it." All great literature bears studying and reading time and time again. This is especially true of the Bible.

There is enough milk in the Bible for the simplest babe to read and to understand. There is also enough meat to challenge the greatest of minds. The reason why man cannot completely master the Bible is that it comes from a mind greater than his. One man remarked, "When I go through the Bible, I feel like someone going to the ocean with a teaspoon. There is so much to get and so little to get it with."

When Sir Walter Scott returned, a trembling invalid from Italy to die in his native land, the sight of his 'sweet home' so invigorated his spirits, that some hope was cherished that he might recover. But he soon relapsed. He found that he must die. Addressing his son-in-law, Lockhart, he said, "Bring me the Book." "What book?" replied Lockhart. "Can you ask," said the expiring genius, whose fascinating novels have charmed the world, but have no balm for death, "Can you ask what book? There is but one—the Holy Bible."[8]

Compared to the millions of other books that have been written, there is only one—the Bible. It is unique, in a class all by itself. The word *Bible* means "book." Even by definition it is "the book." That is another rock that hits the can.

THE BIBLE WORKS IN OUR LIVES

The Bible is true because it works. This is the pragmatic argument: what works is true. Apply principles of the Bible and see if they do not make better husbands, wives, fathers, mothers, sons, daughters, neighbors, employers, employees. See if these principles will not bring a happier life.

There is a manual that goes with a new car and tells how to take care of it: when to change the oil, filters, get lubrications, etc. As long as the owner does what the manual says, he usually gets good service out of the car. If anybody in this world knows what makes that car work and how to keep it working best, it must be the one who built it.

And who would know what is best for men? The one who made him! God has not put man on earth and left him without any direction. He has sent the instruction manual to go with him. He has shown him how to live. He has shown him what life is all about. He has shown him how to relate to other people. He has shown him what to think of himself. He has instructed him on how to spend his time and energy and told him what goals in life are really worth striving for and which are not. Apply these principles and see if they do not work.

The Bible has many hard names in it. It is not the easiest book in the world to read. It has names like Shear-jashub and Mahershalalhashbaz. It might be easier if Bible characters could all have names like Doug, Keith, Sue and Ann. But these people with the strange names were people just like us. The Bible is eternally relevant because it deals with human nature, and human nature has not changed over the centuries. The problems the ancient people wrestled with and the sins with which they were tempted are similar to the ones that confront us.

One can identify with Judas looking at those 30 pieces of silver and saying, "He will probably get away if I betray him. He always has managed to escape. And I do need to make another payment on my new chariot!" There is David up on the roof top peeping over at Bathsheba. "I know I ought to go downstairs and read a book, but maybe one more peep won't hurt. I wonder who she is. Maybe if I just invited her over for lunch to get acquainted, it would be all right."

Look at old Balaam. The Lord told him not to go with the men who were sent by Balak. But Balak offered him great wealth if he would go. It would not hurt to go with him if he only spoke what God told him to. Cain got angry with Abel, his brother, because God accepted Abel's offering. Note how that anger grew into jealousy and hate.

One can see in the lives and mistakes of these Bible personalities material that is relevant today. Apply these principles that the Bible is teaching through examples like this, and, through the instruction that is given, life will be fuller and richer.

A story is told about an atheist who was lecturing in a village in England on his reasons for not believing in God or the Bible. At the conclusion he asked if there were any questions. One elderly lady said she had one. She said, "My husband died 10 years ago and left me with 10 children. It was my faith in the Bible that saw me through those years of hardship, poverty and illness. My faith enabled me to rear my children and make it through those hard times. My question is this: What has your faith done for you?" The lecturer had nothing to say and the assembly ended in confusion.[9]

The Bible is the word of God because it works in our lives. That is another rock that hits the can.

22

One of the most recent of sciences relating to biblical studies is archaeology. Archaeology in itself has not proved that the Bible is inspired. It cannot do that. But archaeology has proved the historical reliability of the biblical account. If a book is inspired, it must be historically reliable. Archaeology has helped to prove the Bible is a reliable history.

In the 19th century it was popular among many critics to discount the reliability of the biblical narratives. Serious doubt was raised as to whether men like Abraham, Isaac and Jacob ever lived. Especially there were doubts if these Biblie characters really did what Genesis said they did. Archaeology has done much to discredit this type of thinking. Even most liberals have been forced to admit the reliability of the biblical accounts.

For example, the Bible mentions the people who lived in the promised land before Israel entered. They were the "Canaanite, Hittite, Hivite, Perizzite, Girgashite, Amorite, and the Jebusite" (Joshua 3:10). For a long time many doubted the references to the Hittites. There was no mention or record of the Hittites in the land of Canaan. Perhaps the writer confused the Amorites with the Hittites. But that is no longer the case. In Cappadocia, in eastern Turkey, recent excavations have turned up the ruins of an ancient and extensive Hittite empire. They had a slanting forehead, a big nose, and their hair was worn in a braid. They may not have been too pretty but they were Hittites!

There is a story in 2 Kings 9 about a king of Israel named Jehu. He was the one who killed Jezebel and wiped out all of the family of Ahab. Archaeology has turned up not only his name, but also his picture.

On the Black Obelisk of Shalmaneser III, Jehu is pictured as bowing before this great Assyrian king. The king calls Jehu by name and even names the tribute brought to him by Jehu. He is the earliest, perhaps the only, Old Testament character with a contemporary portrait of him. It was not one of his better moments, or one of his better poses, but he is there anyway.

In 2 Kings 1:1 it is said that Moab rebelled against Israel. The king of Moab, Mesha, is mentioned in 3:4. The Moabite Stone was discovered in 1868. This stone tells of Moab's rebellion against Israel. The name of Mesha also appears on it. Here is another interesting confirmation of a biblical story.

In 2 Kings 20:20 mention is made of the waterway that Hezekiah constructed in Jerusalem in order to have an ample water supply for the city in case of siege. This waterway is the Siloam Tunnel. In the past century a boy was swimming in the tunnel and noticed some curious writing on one of the walls. He was unable to read it, but it came to the attention of scholars, who deciphered the Siloam Inscription. It was likely put there by Hezekiah. It told of the construction of the tunnel, how the workmen began at each end of the tunnel and met at the middle. It is one of the oldest examples of Hebrew writing and confirms the information about constructing the waterway.

In 2 Kings 19 the story is told about the invasion of Sennacherib. This Assyrian king took all of the fortified cities of Judah and even threatened to take Jerusalem in 701 B.C. He sent his general, the Rabshakeh, to talk Hezekiah into surrendering. Isaiah was sent to tell the king that he did not need to fear Sennacherib's men. The Lord killed 185,000 of his men in one night. He then decided to call off the invasion and return home. One of Sennacherib's monuments, the Taylor Prism, tells of this invasion. Sennacherib boasted of taking the cities of Judah and added that he shut up Hezekiah "like a caged bird." He did not tell of losing 185,000 men, but that is not the type of thing one would want on his monuments. If Sennacherib had succeeded in taking Jerusalem and its king, he would certainly have said so. His statement about shutting up Hezekiah like a bird in a cage is evidence that he did not take the city or capture the king.

The story is told in 2 Kings 25:27 of Evilmerodach, king of Babylon, taking Jehoiachin, king of Judah, out of prison and appointing him a daily ration of food. Near the Ishtar Gate in Babylon a rations list has been found. It tells of the daily portion of oil to be given Jehoiachin of Judah. We have not only evidence of the survival of Jehoiachin, but also an indication as to how much food was given to him and his sons.

One of the most dramatic illustrations of how archaeology has confirmed the Bible is in the story of Sargon. This Assyrian monarch is mentioned in the Bible only in Isaiah 20:1. For a long time it was thought that Isaiah had made a mistake by calling Sargon a king of Assyria. Perhaps he had confused him with some other, or maybe Sargon was only a general under the king. Historians had names and records of all the great kings of Assyria, or so they thought. In 1843 Paul Emile Botta made an astounding discovery at Khorsabad, near Nineveh. He had not enjoyed much success in his work at Nineveh. On a suggestion from one of the workers he went to Khorsabad to try his luck. He uncovered the temple, palace and numerous records of Sargon. He found out why Sargon was not named in the other lists of Assyrian kings. Sargon was a usurper. He took the name *Sargon* after an earlier ruler. Maybe

25

he thought if he had a good name, that would establish his claim to the throne. There is no longer any serious doubt concerning the accuracy of Isaiah 20:1.

Archaeology does not always give what one wants when he wants it. Sometimes there is a bit of a problem harmonizing the archaeological evidence with the Bible, as in the case of the date of the Exodus. But overall, archaeology has been of great help in answering many questions regarding Bible history. A study of archaeology creates a healthy respect for the reliability of the biblical story. Names of people and places, customs, explanations of obscure words—all of these have been provided by archaeology. This is another rock that hits the can!

THE EVIDENCE OF PROPHECY

In Romans 4:17 Paul said that God "calleth those things which be not as though they were" (KJV). Predictions and prophecies in the Bible that were made many years before their fulfillment must be evidence of the hand of God. Fulfillment of prophecy is strong evidence for the inspiration of the Bible.

In Isaiah 44:28 and 45:1 the prophet mentions Cyrus and says that he will accomplish the will of God by letting Israel return home from captivity. That is quite remarkable since Isaiah lived about 700 B.C., and Cyrus was not even born until about 100 years later. He let Israel return home over 150 years after the prophecy was made. Josephus said that Cyrus read of himself in Isaiah and upon that provocation decided to let Israel return home (*Ant.* IX, i, 2). This is doubtful, but Josephus, who wrote slightly after the time of Christ, was impressed with this remarkable prediction. This prediction has led many liberal scholars to suggest that

26

this part of Isaiah was not written by the prophet, but came much later, after Cyrus made his decree. So far there has been no evidence, historically or textually, for such an opinion.

Another remarkable prophecy is Ezekiel 26:3-5. This is the oracle against Tyre. Ezekiel said that Tyre would be broken into, her dust would be scraped from her, she would be made bare like the top of a rock. After this experience the inhabitants of Tyre moved out to an island just off the coast from the old city of Tyre and built a new city of Tyre. The ruins of the old Tyre remained on the coast. Over 200 years later Alexander the Great marched with his army across Asia Minor and turned south through Phoenicia and Palestine. He tried to take the island city of Tyre, but he could not because of the water that separated the island from the mainland. He ordered his troops to scrape the rubble of the old city into the water and built a causeway over to the island. In this way, he took the island. The old city was scraped bare like a rock. It is even today a place for the spreading of nets in the midst of the sea.

There has been some question about this prophecy since some think Ezekiel said that the king of Babylon would scrape the city bare. Later Ezekiel admitted (so some say) that he made a mistake in supposing that Nebuchadnezzar would get the spoil of Tyre (29:19, 20). But Ezekiel did not say that Nebuchadnezzar would take the spoil of Tyre. He predicted that "many nations" would come against Tyre (26:3). The work of Nebuchadnezzar is described in verses 7-11 of chapter 26. Notice that verse 12 changes from *he* to *they*. *They* obviously includes more than Nebuchadnezzar. The statement that many nations would have a part in Tyre's downfall is evidence that Ezekiel did not envision

27

all of this to be done by the king of Babylon. Here is another remarkable example of fulfilled prophecy.

Other examples of fulfilled prophecy could be furnished, but by far the most impressive is the prophecy of Christ through the Old Testament. One powerful element in the preaching of the apostles is the fact that Jesus of Nazareth fulfilled the prophecies of the Old Testament. The fact that the Christ would come through Abraham (Genesis 22:18), Isaac (26:4) and Jacob (28:14) was predicted. He was to descend through the tribe of Judah (49:10) and be of the seed of David (2 Samuel 7:11-14).

His virgin birth was predicted (Isaiah 7:14). Even the place of birth was foretold (Micah 5:2). Many of the events of the earthly ministry were predicted, as the Gospel of Matthew attests time after time. The suffering and death of Jesus were foretold in Isaiah 53 and other places. Even his resurrection was predicted in Psalms 16. The establishment of his church can be seen in Isaiah 2:2-4 and Daniel 2:44.

The thread of prophecy in the Old Testament and its fulfillment in the New is ample proof that this book is the work of a divine hand. The purpose, planning and design for the coming of Christ, and the intricate details of the life of Jesus of Nazareth as predicted centuries beforehand offer proof not only of the deity of Christ, but also of the inspiration of the book that contains these marvelous truths. Here is another rock that hits the can!

You can trust your Bible to be the word of God. There is just too much evidence all pointing in the same direction to deny it. The claims of the Bible, the history of the book, its uniqueness, its working in the lives of those who accept it, the evidence of archaeology and the undeniable evidence of prophecy all unite to proclaim this book is God's Word.

FOOTNOTES

[1]William Paley, *A View of the Evidence of Christianity*, ed. Richard Whately (London, 1859; reprint edition), p. 397.

[2]Scripture quotations are from the New American Standard Version unless otherwise stated.

[3]Thomas Fuller, *The Church History of Britain*, ed. J. S. Brewer (Oxford: University Press, 1945), II, 424.

[4]Cited in Sir Fredric Kenyon, *Our Bible and the Ancient Manuscripts*, rev. A. W. Adams (New York: Harper and Brothers, 1958), p. 289.

[5]"The Fool Hath Said," *Gospel Advocate*, 89 (July 31, 1947), p. 558.

[6]"God's Word," by John Clifford, The Treasury of Religious Verse, Donald Kauffman, comp. (Westwood, N.J.: Fleming H. Revel Co., 1962), p. 49; *Masterpieces of Religious Verse*, ed. James Dalton Morrison (N.Y.: Harper & Bros., 1948), no. 1624.

[7]G. Ernest Wright, *The Challenge of Israel's Faith* (Chicago: The University of Chicago Press, 1944), p. 14.

[8]T. Harrison, *Three Hundred Testimonies in Favor of Religion and the Bible by Distinguished Men and Women* (Cincinnati: Robert Clarke & Co., 1888), p. 340.

[9]"Defeated," *Gospel Advocate*, 91 (May 5, 1949), p. 274.

CHAPTER II
Which Books Belong in the Bible?

Who decided that there should be 66 books in the Bible? There is no verse in the Bible that says, "Behold thou shalt have 66 books in thy Bible." And of course the Bible did not fall from heaven complete with the 66 books and signed by the apostles.

The process by which the 66 books became a part of the Bible is called the history of the canon. This word *canon* comes from a Greek word *kanon,* which means "reed" or "measuring rod." The word came to denote not the measuring stick but that which was measured. That which "passed the test" is the canon. So, the canon is the books that should be in the Bible. Canonicity means acceptance into the canon.

There are three main questions in this study. (1) Do we have all of the books that God intended for us to have? (2) How do we know whether a book should be in the Bible? (3) How did we happen to arrive at the number 66?

DO WE HAVE ALL OF THE BOOKS?

There are many books mentioned in the Bible that are not in existence today. In Numbers 21, where the children of Israel are journeying on the way to the

31

plains of Moab, there is a mention of "the Book of the Wars of Jehovah" (vs. 14-15). It is most likely a history book telling of Israel in the wilderness.

Two references are made to the Book of Jashar. The story of Joshua commanding the sun to stand still is recorded in "the Book of Jashar." Also the lament of David for Saul and Jonathan could be found in this lost book, "Behold, it is written in the book of Jashar" (2 Samuel 1:18). The word *Jashar* means "upright one." It could be the name of a man, or it could be "The Book of the Upright One." Whichever it may be and whoever may be the author, here is one book mentioned in the Bible that has been lost. The Rosacrucian Order does have a book among their works called the Book of Jashar, but it is obviously not the one mentioned in the Old Testament.

There is a lost history book of the reign of Solomon. 1 Kings 11:41 states: "Now the rest of the acts of Solomon, and whatever he did, and his wisdom, are they not written in the Book of the Acts of Solomon?" There is no such book today. Most likely this is a court record of the days of Solomon that has long been lost. This book may have served as a source for the stories about Solomon in Kings.

Similarly, 1 Chronicles 29:29 mentions three books that tell about the days of David: "Now the acts of King David from first to last, are written in the Chronicles of Samuel the seer, in the Chronicles of Nathan the prophet and in the Chronicles of Gad the seer." Samuel, Nathan and Gad are three prophets who lived in the time of David and figured from time to time in the life of this king. It is highly unlikely that the book of Samuel the seer could be the canonical 1 and 2 Samuel; there are no such books today as the book of Nathan or the book of Gad.

There is another mention of the book of Nathan, along with some other "lost books" of antiquity, in 2 Chronicles 9:29:

> Now the rest of the acts of Solomon, from the first to last, are they not written in the records of Nathan the prophet, and in the prophecy of Ahijah the Shilonite, and in the visions of Iddo the seer concerning Jeroboam the son of Nebat?

In the book of Kings there are frequent references to the chronicles of the kings of Judah or of Israel. For example 1 Kings 14:29 says, "Now the rest of the acts of Rehoboam and all that he did, are they not written in the Book of the Chronicles of the King of Judah?" Compare also 1 Kings 14:19, "Now the rest of the acts of Jeroboam, how he made war and how he reigned, behold, they are written in the Book of the Chronicles of the King of Israel." The first impulse is to think that these refer to 1 and 2 Chronicles. These are not the ones referred to. These books of chronicles are probably court records. The inspired writer is saying that if any one wants to know more about the particular kings, he can check the court records; that is all that he sees fit to say about them. There is good reason to believe that court records of the reigns of kings were kept. In Esther 2:23 and 6:1 Ahasuerus, king of Persia, kept such records. These chronicles were secular history books that the inspired writer may have used as a source in his work.

In the story of the death of Josiah, king of Judah, the chronicler said, "Then Jeremiah chanted a lament for Josiah. And all the male and female singers speak about Josiah in their lamentations to this day. And they made them an ordinance in Israel; behold, they are also written in the Lamentations" (2 Chronicles 35:25).

Naturally one would think that this is the book of Lamentations which follows Jeremiah in the Bible. But again, there is no reference to the death of Josiah in this biblical book. This book of Lamentations must be some book by Jeremiah that has been lost.

There are also some "lost books" in the New Testament. The Corinthian correspondence mentions one and probably another letter by Paul to Corinth that has been lost. Paul said in 1 Corinthians 5:9, "I wrote you in my letter not to associate with immoral people." Some have suggested that this letter is preserved in 2 Corinthians 6:14-7:1, but this raises more problems than it solves. How did it get to be a part of 2 Corinthians?

Also in 2 Corinthians 2:4 Paul mentions a letter he had written to the church at Corinth "out of much affliction and anguish of heart." This does not sound like 1 Corinthians. Perhaps this is yet another "lost letter" by Paul to the Corinthians. It has been styled the "sorrowful letter." So there may be at least two letters that Paul wrote to Corinth that have been lost. Again there has been an attempt to find this letter among the Corinthian correspondence. Some have proposed that it is chapters 10-13 of 2 Corinthians; but as in the other case, this raises more problems than it solves.

As he closes out his letter to the Colossians, Paul tells them, "And when this letter is read among you, have it also read in the church of the Laodiceans; and you, for your part read my letter that is coming from Laodicea" (4:16). There is no letter of Paul to Laodicea. Some have suggested that it is Ephesians; others, that it is Philemon. But it is more likely a letter by Paul that has been lost.

There are many writings mentioned in the Bible

which have been lost. Suppose one of these is found. Should it be put into the Bible?

Does the church need everything the apostles wrote? There are many things that the apostles wrote which have not been preserved: grocery lists, laundry lists, maybe even old sermon notes or outlines. Certainly in his lifetime James wrote more things than just the five chapters in the book that bears his name. There are probably many letters of Paul that have not been preserved. And what about writings of Andrew, Philip, Bartholomew, Thomas, etc.?

The revelation in the Bible is very selective. If one should write a story of the creation of the universe, he would probably do it in several volumes. God did it in one or two chapters in Genesis. Even so the Gospels do not intend to tell everything that Jesus did. John admitted this fact in his gospel (20:30). He continued by saying that if everything that Jesus did were written down, "I suppose that even the world itself would not contain the books which were written" (21:25).

Really, the Acts of the Apostles is not a good name for this book. It would be more fitting to call it "Some of the acts of some of the apostles," especially only two—Peter and Paul.

The same reserve is seen in the selection of the writings for the canon. In his wisdom God has preserved only the essential messages and letters of the apostles. Christians would like to know much more about many things in the Bible, but God has given all that is necessary to know. It would be good to have many more writings of the apostles and other inspired men, but in the books preserved there is all that is necessary for one to know and understand in order to enter into eternal life.

Of course, if in the sands of Egypt, or elsewhere, an authentic writing of an inspired man should come to light, it could easily be included in the canon. Inspiration does not contradict itself; there should be no fear that it may contradict the truth already revealed. But again, there is no need for further writings. As in providing for salvation, so also in revealing that salvation, God has granted "everything pertaining to life and godliness" (2 Peter 1:3).

HOW DO WE KNOW WHETHER OR NOT A BOOK SHOULD BE IN THE BIBLE?

The second big question in this chapter is how can one tell whether or not a book ought to be in the Bible. One of the main tests is that of authorship. If a man was inspired when he spoke, certainly he would also be inspired when he wrote. The writings of Peter should be just as authoritative as his sermons were. Very early in the church the words of the apostles were regarded as inspired. Anything written by the apostles was readily accepted. The writings of Matthew and John were accepted because the writers were apostles. Luke was accepted because of his connection with Paul, and Mark because of his connection with Peter. James, the brother of the Lord, was called an apostle in Galatians 1:19. If he is the author of the book of James, this book also should be accepted. Likewise, if the author of Jude is also a brother of the Lord, his writings would be accepted.

But there is one book in the New Testament that got into the canon even though the author was unknown—the book of Hebrews. When the New Testament canon was being finalized, in the fourth century, there was a great effort to make Paul the author of Hebrews in order to have it included.

But besides that of authorship, there is another factor that helped decide the canon, the intrinsic worth of the book. Literature is something so well-written that future generations will not let it die. Similarly a work like Hebrews is one that speaks with the authority of a New Testament apostle. Its message is in harmony with the other books of the New Testament. Its lessons were vitally needed by the early church. The early Christians recognized their need of this book and its intrinsic worth. They would not discard this work even if the authorship was uncertain.

The gap between the canonical and the non-canonical books is so wide, the difference is so clear, that it is easy to tell which books should be rejected. There is the Old Testament Apocrypha. There were also works (such as the *Gospel of Thomas*, the *Acts of Pilate* and the *Acts of Peter*) that tried to make it into the New Testament. These apocryphal books are so inferior to the canonical works that comparison will show why they were rejected.

Look for a moment at the *Gospel of Thomas*. This work attempts to tell of Jesus when he was a child. It was probably written in the fourth century A.D. It tells of the time when Jesus, at the age of five, made clay sparrows out of the mud. He was rebuked for doing this on the Sabbath. Jesus said to the clay sparrows, "Rise and take you flight." They all came to life and flew away.

One day Jesus' mother sent him down to get some water from the well, and he dropped the pitcher and broke it. He took off his coat, filled it with water and brought home a coat full of water to his mother. One time a little boy was running past him and hit him. Jesus turned to him and said, "You will not finish your course." The child fell dead at Jesus' word. No parent would want his child playing with someone like that!

Another story in the *Gospel of Thomas* tells about a little boy who fell off a roof and died. His mother accused Jesus of killing her son. Jesus, who was still on the roof, jumped down to the ground and said to the dead boy, "Arise Zeno, tell your mother if I killed you." The boy rose and said to his mother, "No, he did not kill me, but verily he has made me alive."

Jesus helped his father in the carpenter shop. One day when Joseph was making a bed for a rich man, he had sawed the board too short. Jesus had his father hold one end of the board and he held the other end. He pulled the board to the desired length. He would be a handy helper for any carpenter.[1]

When compared with the canonical Gospels, Matthew, Mark, Luke and John, it is obvious why these apocryphal works were not accepted. The four in the New Testament are so superior to the apocryphal gospels that there is really no question.

There are earlier works that are found in some New Testament manuscripts. These for a while were accepted by some early Christians as part of Scripture: *Epistle of Barnabas, I Clement, Shepherd of Hermas.* But these never were seriously considered as part of Scripture. They were not written by apostles and do not carry the ring of authority that the apostles' works have. Some even have erroneous teachings in them. *I Clement* uses for proof of the resurrection the story of the phoenix bird that comes to life every 500 years. The *Shepherd of Hermas* has some rather racy parts in it. The author gives an insight into his past life. In fact, Tertullian called him "The Apocryphal Shepherd of Adulterers" (*De Pud.* X). The *Epistle of Barnabas* is made out to be written by Barnabas, the companion of

Paul. But this has been disproved. A work that is untruthful about its authorship could not be trusted implicitly in other matters.

HOW DID WE ARRIVE AT THE NUMBER 66 FOR BOOKS OF THE BIBLE?

The books of the Bible were written for specific purposes to fulfill specific needs. Although the writers recognized that they were writing through the guidance of the Holy Spirit, they did not write these books simply to put another one in the Bible. John did not sit down to write and say, "I think I will write 2 and 3 John today. We need two short books like that in the New Testament." No, he was writing to a specific church (or lady) and to a specific individual, Gaius. He had something to say to these parties. Only later were these letters preserved and included in a collection that became the New Testament.

When Paul wrote Philemon, he was trying to get Philemon to receive back Onesimus, a slave who had run away from him. The fact that this small letter should be a book in the New Testament possibly did not cross the mind of Paul at the time. When he wrote 1 Corinthians, he did not say, "I've just added another book to the New Testament today." He was trying to straighten out some problems in the church at Corinth.

These early Christians realized the value of these books and kept them. They refused to let them die because their message was to all Christians, not just the individuals to whom they were addressed.

But most likely the very early Christians did not attach too much importance to keeping their letters. Why should they keep letters from the apostles when they could talk to them face to face? Only when these apostles began to die and their word became scarce was there a conscious effort to preserve every communication from them.

I get letters from my mother every week. I do not keep them. After reading them, I throw them away, knowing I will get another one next week. But if I thought one particular letter might be the last one I would ever receive from her, I would keep it and treasure it. So, while the apostles were alive, the Christians probably did not think about keeping and treasuring their writings.

Another factor was the belief that the Lord's return would be immediate. Many of the early Christians thought that the Lord would return in their lifetime. They saw no need for preserving writings for future generations. As generations began to come and go, the early Christians saw that they would be on this earth for some time and began to search about for the works of the apostles to guide them in their work and life.

The process by which the 66 books came into the Bible is an interesting topic. The Jews divided the Old Testament into three parts: law, prophets and writings. Jesus alluded to this threefold division of the Jewish Scriptures in Luke 24:44: ". . . all things which are written about Me in the Law of Moses and the Prophets and the Psalms must be fulfilled." Notice that the law and prophets were mentioned. The third division Jesus called the Psalms, which is the largest book in that part of the Bible.

The law, according to the ancient Jews, was accorded the highest degree of canonicity and was accepted first. This law comprises the five books of Moses, Genesis through Deuteronomy. Second came the prophets.

They were divided, not into major and minor, but into former and latter. The former prophets were Joshua, Judges, Samuel and Kings. Originally Samuel and Kings were one book each. The latter prophets were Isaiah, Jeremiah, Ezekiel and the Book of the Twelve (minor prophets). The third category was the last section of the Old Testament to be closed. It was called the writings; the Greek term is *Hagiographa*, which means "holy writings." This is a sort of catch-all. It contains the books of poetry, Psalms, Job and Proverbs. Five short books are found in this section; they are the five Megilloth (scrolls): Song of Solomon, Ruth, Lamentations, Ecclesiastes and Esther. The last three are Daniel, Ezra-Nehemiah (considered as one book) and Chronicles. In Matthew 23:35 Jesus said that all the righteous blood would come upon his generation, from the blood of Abel to Zechariah. He could be referring to the death of Zechariah in 2 Chronicles 24:20-22. Abel, in Genesis and Zechariah in 2 Chronicles would represent the first and last books of the Hebrew Bible; in other words, from one end to the other. There is one problem, however. The Zechariah mentioned by Jesus in Matthew 23 was the son of Berechiah, and the one killed in 2 Chronicles 24 was the son of Jehoiada. So these may not be the same person.

Josephus, the Jewish historian of about A.D. 90, said there were 22 books in the Hebrew Bible, to correspond with the 22 letters of the Hebrew alphabet (*Against Apion* I, 8). Josephus considered the 12 minor prophets to be one book, he also counted the books of Samuel, Kings and Chronicles as one book each and combined Ezra and Nehemiah into one book. That would make 24 books. The number 24 is the usual one given by the Jews for the number of books

41

in their Bible. Probably Josephus placed Ruth under Judges and Lamentations under Jeremiah to come up with his 22.

There was serious doubt over five books in the Old Testament. One of these was Esther because it did not contain the name of God. A second was Ecclesiastes because its tone was so pessimistic. But the pessimism in Ecclesiastes is only in the life away from God. The author is showing the futility of life apart from God. A third book was Proverbs. Chapter 26:4, 5 seems to contradict itself. Verse four says do not answer a fool according to his folly, and verse five says answer him according to his folly. There is no contradiction here. Two different lessons are being taught. There are times to answer a fool according to his folly, and there are times not to.

A fourth book was the Song of Solomon. It was rejected because it was too sensual. A love poem like this, they thought, could have no place in the Scriptures. It was considered to be an allegory of God's love for his people and so was accepted. But really, there is nothing wrong with a book in the Bible dealing with such a vital part of life. There is nothing wrong with the physical aspect of life. Love between a man and a woman is something beautiful and pleasant. God made man and woman, and the attraction of one for the other is a natural thing. Under the guidelines that God has laid down, there is nothing at all wrong with delight in the physical love. This book can be accepted just as it is. All of the shame and embarrassment associated with sex comes from an abuse of the place that God has given it. The Song of Solomon puts it in its right place.

The fifth book to be seriously questioned is Ezekiel. The main problem is the temple in Ezekiel's vision in chapters 40-48. This structure was never built, so some said Ezekiel must have been a false prophet. The Talmud tells of a Hananiah ben Hezekiah who burned 300 jars of oil trying to harmonize Ezekiel's temple with the temple in Jerusalem in order to save the book for the canon (*Hagigah* 13a). Really, he could have saved himself the trouble if he had only realized that Ezekiel's vision was never intended to have a literal fulfillment. Ezekiel wrote in figurative style. His figurative language was never intended to be taken literally. He even told of a spring of water that would turn the Dead Sea into fresh water. When Ezekiel is taken as the prophet intended his book to be understood, there is no problem.

Like the threefold development of the Old Testament canon, the New Testament canon also developed in three stages: the Gospels, the letters of Paul and the general epistles. The four Gospels were very early accepted as genuine. The words of Jesus were precious to the early church, and their best source of these was in the four Gospels. Before A.D. 200 there is evidence that the letters of Paul were collected. In the fourth century the New Testament canon was rounded out by the inclusion of the general epistles and Revelation.

There were three main factors that led to the formation of the New Testament canon. The first of these was the heretical canon drawn up by Marcion about A.D. 140. This false teacher accepted only 10 epistles of Paul and a mutilated Gospel of Luke. He rejected the whole Old Testament. As an answer to this heretical canon, the early Christians made known publicly the canon they were using. Probably the Muratorian Fragment (the earliest extant orthodox canon list, from about A.D. 170) was drawn up to serve this purpose.

43

A second factor was persecution. Under the Roman emperors such as Diocletian it was a death penalty to be found in possession of a copy of Christian scriptures. This brought up the question of which writings were worth dying for. Many uninspired Christian writings were no doubt burned. Only those most precious books would be preserved. Probably several copies of the *Shepherd of Hermas* and other such works were destroyed at this time.

The third factor was the rise of the codex form. In earlier days the Scriptures were written on scrolls. These scrolls were kept in large jars. Inspired and uninspired writings could be kept in the same jar without any problem. But the early Christians adopted the codex form or book form. Instead of rolling up the leaves on a stick, they sewed one edge of these leaves together to make a book. It would be easier to get from the front to the back of the book. If one had a scroll of the Psalms and wanted to turn from the 1st to the 150th Psalm, it would take quite a while. But with the codex form one could turn to the back from the front in a few seconds.

When the codex form became popular, the question arose as to which books should be sewed together. Scrolls of uninspired books could be kept in the jar right beside the canonical ones, but they were omitted when the scribes began to sew the canonical books into a book form.

By the fourth century A.D. the New Testament canon was pretty well set. Those books to be regarded as canonical stood head and shoulders above the ones not admitted. The first list of the 27 books such as are in the New Testament today, with no additions or subtractions, was that of the Festal Letter of Athanasius in A.D. 367. Later in the same century the council of Carthage issued the same list. This council, or any other council, did not decree what books the church had to accept. It simply listed the books that the church already accepted. These books had earned the right to be in the canon. They were written by inspired men, their worth was readily perceived by the early church, and in the providence of God they were kept for them, but not only for *them*—for *all Christians* through the ages.

EXCURSUS: THE OLD TESTAMENT APOCRYPHA

The word *Apocrypha* means "hidden." These are books that appeared between the Old and New Testament and were supposedly "hidden" for a time and now, some say, should be included in the Bible. Some of these works bear the names of men who lived in Old Testament days. There was a strong tradition among the Jews that inspiration ceased in the days of Artaxerxes, king of Persia. This would be about the time of Nehemiah or Malachi, 400 B.C. (See Josephus, *Against Apion* I, 8.) Therefore, in order to get into the Old Testament, books had to be written by men who lived before 400 B.C.

If some man who lived in the period between the Testaments wanted to get a work of his accepted, he would do better not to put his own name on it. He would write it under the name of one such as Jeremiah or Ezra and play like this was an ancient document that had been "hidden" for years and was just now dis-covered. People would get excited about it and think it was the real thing. Of course, this was dishonest, but these were called "pious frauds." After all, if the truth was taught, what matter did it make any way? The New Testament also had apocryphal works. These were written one or two

45

hundred years after the time of Christ under the names of men like Peter, Thomas, or some other notable apostle.

Some of the Old Testament Apocrypha are set forth as "additions" to canonical books. There are additions to Esther. Two or three short works are supposed to be additions to Daniel. These, supposedly, are parts of the books that originally belonged in the canonical works, but were lost out; now they should be reinserted in their proper places.

Apocryphal works usually attempt to supply information that is missing in the canonical books. For example, the Bible does not tell what the three Hebrew children were doing in the fiery furnace. The additions to Daniel tell of their prayer and song while in the furnace. 2 Chronicles 33 tells about the repentance of the wicked king Manasseh; verse 18 makes special mention of his prayer. Manasseh's prayer was not preserved in the Bible, so the Apocrypha supplies the prayer of Manasseh. The only story of the childhood of Jesus after his return to Nazareth is in Luke 2:41-52, where he was lost in the temple. The Apocryphal *Gospel of Thomas* supplies all sorts of stories of the miracles and exploits of the child Jesus.

Here are the books that comprise the Old Testament Apocrypha, along with a brief summary of each of them.

First and Second Esdras. Esdras is the Greek spelling of Ezra. These works are purported to be written by Ezra. Since Ezra lived before 400 B.C. it would be easy to consider him an inspired writer. First and Second Esdras were written in order to explain the days that are to come. One of the main points in Esdras is the coming of the Son of Man and the visions of these days.

Tobit. The book of Tobit begins by telling about a very pious Jew, Tobit, who buried one of his country-men lest he suffer the disgrace of lying unburied. Because he had contact with the dead, Tobit was unclean and had to sleep outside that night. As he slept, bird droppings fell into his eyes and blinded him.

There was a deposit of money that Tobit had left with a kinsman of his named Gabael, who lived in Media. Tobit sent his son, Tobias, to go and get the money. A companion went with Tobias on this trip; he was the angel Raphael in disguise. On their journey, Tobias and his friend came to a river where a fish jumped out and tried to swallow Tobias' foot. Raphael advised Tobias to catch the fish. They ate part of it but kept the heart, liver and gall.

When they arrived at Media, Tobias fell in love with Raguel's daughter, Sarah. Sarah had been given in marriage to seven men, but the wicked demon Asmodaeus had killed them all. Raphael told Tobias to place the fish's liver and heart on smoking incense; this stench would drive away the demon forever. The smell from the fish drove the demon into Upper Egypt, where Raphael followed him and bound him hand and foot.

After the wedding feast, and after having received the 10 talents of silver from Gabael, Tobias, Sarah and Raphael returned to Tobit. When Tobit stumbled out to meet his son, Tobias sprinkled the fish gall into his eyes, and the blind man received his sight.

Judith. Holofernes was commander-in-chief of the armies of Nebuchadnezzar, king of Assyria. He laid siege to Samaria. Judith, a devout Jewish widow, went out to Holofernes under the guise of giving him important information. She refused to eat the food that was offered her because it did not conform to Jewish food laws. On the fourth day Holofernes gave a great banquet and invited Judith. Hot with wine and passion, Holofernes commanded all of his servants to leave the room. While Holofernes lay on his bed in a drunken stupor, Judith took his sword and cut off his head. She placed the head in her food bag and returned to her people. Judith showed her people the head of Holofernes and inspired them to fight against the Assyrians. The Assyrians were thrown into a panic and were soundly defeated by Israel.

Additions to Esther. The book of Esther had a hard time being accepted into the Old Testament canon because it did not contain the name of God. Although the hand of God in his providential care of his people is evident throughout the book, his name does not appear. Could any book that did not even have God's name in it be a part of God's Word?

Remember that apocryphal works tend to supply missing information, details that the canonical works do not have. The apocryphal additions to Esther contain scores of references to the name of God. When one includes these additions to Esther, there is no longer any question about the name of God being present. For example, look at the prayer of Mordecai in Addition 13:9ff.: "O Lord, Lord, King who rulest over all . . . thou art Lord of all, and there is no one who can resist thee, who art Lord. . . . And now, O Lord God and King, God of Abraham, spare thy people."[2] There is no vital information supplied by these additions to Esther. The main value is the inclusion of the name of God.

Wisdom of Solomon. The Wisdom of Solomon has some interesting and helpful proverbs that sound very much like the canonical book of Proverbs. This is probably one of the best, quality-wise, of the apocryphal books.

Ecclesiasticus. Ecclesiasticus, not to be confused with the canonical Ecclesiastes, is also called the wisdom of Sirach, or Ben Sira. It is an excellent work similar to Proverbs and Ecclesiastes. It probably was written about the third century B.C.

Baruch and The Letter of Jeremiah. Baruch was Jeremiah's secretary (Jeremiah 45:1). This apocryphal work was probably written about A.D. 70, when Jerusalem was destroyed. In the time of Baruch (586 B.C.) Jerusalem was destroyed by the Babylonians. This book was written when the city fell to the Romans about 650 years later, but it was written as if it were in the days of Jeremiah.

The Letter of Jeremiah was probably written about the same time as the book of Baruch. It points out the folly of idolatry.

Additions to Daniel. There are several small works that are supposed to be included with the canonical Daniel. They supply information about the work of Daniel and also supplement stories in Daniel. They are: the Song of the Three Holy Children, Susanna and Bel and the Dragon.

1. *The Song of the Three Holy Children.* As mentioned earlier, the song of the three Hebrew children contains the prayer and song of these three while in the fiery furnace. This is an attempt to supplement one of the canonical stories in Daniel (chapter 3).

2. *Susanna.* The story of Susanna shows Daniel's ability as a detective. Susanna's husband was Joakim, a Jew of great wealth and honor. He had a garden which was a favorite meeting place for the Jews. Two of the elders were inflamed with passion for Susanna as they saw her walking in the garden. One day they played as if they were leaving but retraced their steps and hid in the garden. When she thought the gates were locked, Susanna went down to the garden to bathe. When Susanna was alone, the two elders came from their hiding and tried to get Susanna to

consent to their wishes. If she did not, they said they would swear that they had found her being intimate with a young man.

Susanna cried for help, and the elders likewise cried out with their story. When Susanna was tried, the judges tended to believe the testimony of the two elders. Daniel asked permission to question the elders separately. He asked each one under what tree did he see Susanna and the young man. The elders named different trees, and their testimony was shown to be false. Susanna was found innocent, and the two elders were put to death.

3. *Bel and the Dragon.* Bel and the Dragon also shows Daniel's ability as a detective. There was a great idol called Bel which the people worshipped. They would place large quantities of food beside the idol, lock up the temple and return the next day to find the food consumed. They concluded that the idol was alive and ate the food. One night Daniel checked this out. Before leaving the idol, Daniel spread a layer of ashes on the ground inside the temple. The next morning the food was gone as usual, but footprints in the ashes led to a secret entrance through which the priests had been entering and consuming the food themselves. Thus the mystery of the "live idol" was exposed.

There was also a great dragon (snake) that many of the people worshipped. Daniel made up a concoction of pitch, fat and hair and fed it to the dragon. He swelled up and burst. Daniel said, "See what you have been worshipping."

The Prayer of Manasseh. Probably the most wicked king of Judah was Manasseh. 2 Chronicles 33:12-16 tells of his repentance in his old age. It also mentions his famous prayer in verse 18. This prayer does not appear in the canonical books, so the Apocrypha provides that prayer. The Prayer of Manasseh is a beautiful, though rather brief, prayer. There is, however, very little evidence to lead one to believe that it came from the time of Manasseh.

First and Second Maccabees. First and Second Maccabees are histories of the Maccabean era. They tell of the revolt of the Jews against the Syrians in 165 B.C. The Jewish heroes of this rebellion were the Maccabees. They gained religious independence for Judah, and later, political independence. First Maccabees is a very reliable history. Second Maccabees is not thought to be quite so reliable.

These are the books of the Apocrypha. There is no crucial doctrine relating to the Christian faith that is found in these books and not found in the canonical books. Whether the Apocrypha is included or omitted, the Christian message remains the same.

There is another group of religious writings produced by the Jewish people between the Testaments. They have never been accepted by any Christian group, not even the Roman Catholic Church. They are called the Pseudepigrapha; this word means "false writings." One work in the Pseudepigrapha, the Book of Enoch, is quoted in Jude 14, 15. But even here there is no evidence that any of the apostles considered these works as canonical.

The question arises, "Why is the Apocrypha not accepted into the canon?" A more pertinent question would be, "Why *should* the Apocrypha be accepted into the canon?"

There are four positions regarding the Apocrypha. The Roman church adopted all of the Apocrypha except 1 and 2 Esdras and the Prayer of Manasseh at the fourth session of the Council of Trent on

April 8, 1546. They call the Apocrypha deutero-canonical (second canon). A second attitude toward the Apocrypha is seen in the Greek Catholic Church. As of yet they have not made a decision regarding the canonicity of the Apocrypha. Thirdly, the Church of England does not regard the Apocrypha as canonical but places it on a level above the writings of the church fathers. Fourthly, the Westminister Confession of Faith, which is representative of the Protestant churches, says that the Apocrypha is of no authority in the church of God nor to be otherwise approved or made use of other than as human writing.

One main argument given for including the Apocrypha is that Jesus and the apostles used the Septuagint, the Greek translation of the Old Testament made about 200 B.C. In copies of the Septuagint, Apocryphal works are frequently found. Since Jesus placed his approval on the Septuagint by his use of it, he must have approved the canon of the Septuagint, which contained the Apocrypha.

There, however, is no real evidence that the books of the Apocrypha were found in the Septuagint in the days of Jesus. The earliest extant copies of the Septuagint date from the fourth century A.D. How can one be sure that copies of the Septuagint 300 years earlier contained the Apocrypha? These fourth century manuscripts also have other non-canonical works in them such as *1 and 2 Clement*, the *Epistle of Barnabas*, and the *Shepherd of Hermas*. By the same logic one would have to consider these as canonical also.

The Jews did not accept the Apocrypha; even today they do not accept these books as canonical. Jesus never quoted the Apocrypha in the Gospels. In fact, no New Testament book quotes from the

Apocrypha. The early church fathers almost unanimously refused to include the Apocrypha. Even Jerome refused the Apocrypha. He was commissioned to produce an accepted Latin translation of the Scriptures about A.D. 400. This work of Jerome, the Vulgate, became the standard text for the Catholics. But Jerome refused to include the Apocrypha as part of his translation of the Old Testament.

The Roman Catholic Church decreed that all of the Apocrypha except 1 and 2 Esdras and the Prayer of Manasseh should be considered as part of the canon. One wonders why the Roman Church did not take all of the Apocrypha instead of all but these three.

Some of the stories in the Apocrypha are hard to accept as coming from the hand of God. The additions to Daniel and the book of Tobit do not sound like the miracle stories of the canonical works. Admittedly, this is a subjective judgment, but the stories of the Scriptures seem to be on a higher plane than these in the Apocrypha.

One scripture (Maccabees 12:42) mentions praying for the dead. This has been used as a proof test for the doctrine of purgatory. If one can pray for the dead, they must be in a place where they can be helped spiritually. Therefore, there must be a purgatory. But even here the dead for whom prayers are offered were guilty of mortal sin, idolatry; prayer could not save those who died in this type of sin.

The fact that the Jews, the apostles, Jesus himself, the writers of the New Testament and the early church fathers did not use the Apocrypha as canonical is strong evidence against accepting them into the canon.[3]

FOOTNOTES

[1]This and other similar works can be found in *The Apocryphal New Testament*, tr. Montague Rhodes James (Oxford: The Clarendon Press, 1924).

[2]*The Apocrypha of the Old Testament*, Revised Standard Version (New York: Thomas Nelson & Sons, 1957), p. 83.

[3]An excellent treatment of why the Apocrypha should not be accepted into the canon is in Floyd Filson, *Which Books Belong in the Bible?* (Philadelphia: Westminster Press, 1957).

CHAPTER III
Is the Biblical Text Reliable?

The question of canonicity is known as Higher Criticism. The problem of restoring the original reading in the books is called Lower Criticism. Higher Criticism deals with authorship and the authority of a book. Lower Criticism raises the question, "How do we know that we have an exact copy of the book? How can we be sure that some scribe has not changed the original reading?"

THE MAKING OF ANCIENT BOOKS

There were various types of writing materials used by ancient people. The Ten Commandments were written on stone. Some ancient documents were written on clay with a pen called a stylus. It had a wedge-shaped tip to make the wedge-shaped characters called cuneiform writing. Broken pieces of pottery (ostraca) have been found with writing on them. These ostraca seem to have served as their scrap paper. Most likely the books of the Bible were first written on animal skins, leather or parchment scrolls. It is probable that some of the New Testament books were written on papyrus. Papyrus came from the plant by that name that grew in Egypt. The stalk would be cut into strips and the

55

strips would be pasted together to make a writing surface. The smooth side generally used for writing was called the *recto*. The rougher back side, used only when there was no more room to write, was called the *verso*. These materials were perishable in a damp climate. But papyrus dating from 400 B.C. has been unearthed from the hot dry sands of Egypt.

Of course, there were no printing presses in those days. All of the reproduction of books was done by hand. Professionals who spent their lives in reproducing written materials were called scribes. Because of the scarcity of written copies often the scribes would assemble in one room, called a scriptorium. The reader would read out a line from the manuscript, and each scribe would then copy down that line. The scribes did not sit at desks. They would often sit on the floor and cross their legs, hold their palette on their lap and write. Often notations in the margins of the manuscripts show the human side of these scribes. One wrote, "It's cold today," another, Well, I call this vellum thin." One of the most interesting is this one found in many non-biblical manuscripts: "He who does not know how to write supposes it to be no labor; but though only three fingers write, the whole body labors."[1]

This type of reproduction was very expensive. Copies of the Scriptures were quite scarce. Probably most churches had copies of only a few books. Also, this type of reproduction led to errors in the text. All copies have errors in them because of the human element. A later scribe would reproduce the first scribe's errors and add some of his own. A third copyist would reproduce the errors of the first two and add some of his own. In this process, many errors could creep into the text.

Perhaps it is good that the original copies of the

biblical books have been lost because someone would be wanting to worship them. Only copies of copies of copies of the originals are extant. Lower criticism aims at restoring the original reading of the text, working through the errors in the manuscripts, and trying to decide which of the variant readings was the original one.

UNINTENTIONAL CHANGES

Some of the errors are errors in writing. As in English, so in Hebrew and Greek, some of the letters look very much alike. Some variant readings are the result of the confusion of letters. One excellent example of this is in 1 Samuel 12:11. Samuel listed some of the judges that ruled over Israel. Among these were Jerubbaal (Gideon), Bedan and Jephthah. Gideon and Jephthah are well known, but who is Bedan? There is no Bedan in the Scriptures. This obviously is a corruption of Barak. Other versions give the reading here as Barak. In Hebrew Bedan is written בדן, and Barak is written ברק. A weary scribe could easily convert *Barak* into *Bedan*. A similar problem can be seen in 1 Timothy 3:16, where there is confusion between two Greek letters that give variant readings: either "God was manifested in the flesh" or "who was manifested in the flesh" (Θ = "God," Ο = "who").

Another type of scribal error is wrong word division. In the ancient scriptures the letters and words are all run together with no punctuation or other separation. This is one reason why most ancient people read aloud. They had to in order to make sense out of it. Note that Philip ran to the chariot and *heard* the eunuch reading (Acts 8:30). Variant readings because of different word division can be seen in Amos 6:2.

Some versions read, "Will one plow the sea with oxen?" while others read, "Will one plow there with oxen?" The difference is in the word division. If the letters ΰʸ7Р11 are taken as one word, the reading is, "Will one plow with oxen?" But if the letters are divided into two words (ΰʸ 7Р11) then the reading is, "Will one plow the sea with an ox?"

Any typist can appreciate some of the scribal errors such as metathesis. This is reversing the position of two letters. One excellent example of variant readings as the result of metathesis is Mark 14:65. Some manuscripts read *Ἔλαβον* and others, *Ἔβαλον*. If the first reading is used, the reading is "they received him." If the second, it reads, "they cast him." That is why some versions read, "They received him with blows" (NASV) and other versions read, "Set upon him with blows" (NEB).

Two common scribal errors are dittography and haplography. Dittography is repeating a section; haplography is omitting a part of the passage. This often occurs when two lines begin in the same way or end in the same way. It would be easy for a tired scribe to let his eyes jump to the wrong line and continue copying.

Often several scribes would be in the same room, a scriptorium, and one reader would read a line while the others copied it down. There is evidence of variations in texts from faulty hearing. One such example is Revelation 1:5. The KJV reads, "Unto him that . . . washed us." The NASV reads, "To him who released us from our sins." The Greek words for *wash (louo)* and *release (luo)* are pronounced almost the same. When the reader called out the word, some scribes wrote down "wash," and others wrote "loose."

When a scribe was making a copy of the scriptures

from two different ancient manuscripts, what would he do when his two witnesses disagreed? He was not qualified to decide which is the correct reading, and he certainly did not want to leave out anything that should be included. Often he would put both readings into his text. This is called a conflation. At least the scribe preserved the original reading, though he did not know which one was the original. One example of conflation is Luke 24:53. Some manuscripts read "blessing God," and others read "praising God." Some later manuscripts read "praising and blessing God."

INTENTIONAL CHANGES

Some times there were intentional changes in the texts. The scribe would often intentionally change a reading in one of the Gospels to make it agree with the other Gospels. He thought he was doing the readers a favor! It is the general opinion of textual critics to regard as genuine the readings in the Gospels that seem to contradict each other.

At times a scribe would come upon a reading that he knew was erroneous. He did not want to reproduce the error, and so he tried to determine what was the original reading. On the spur of the moment he became a textual critic and tried to solve the problem himself. He may have succeeded, but also he may have made matters worse. That is why it is a general rule to regard as genuine the reading that would explain all of the variations. Sometimes one can see just what changes the scribe made, and where he went wrong.

There are instances where scribes intentionally changed the reading in order to clarify some doctrinal point. If he could get his idea into the Scriptures, that would give it some authority. After all, since his doctrine is the correct one, there is no harm in slipping it into the text, is there? 1 John 5:7, 8 is a good example here. The KJV reads: "For there are three that bear witness in heaven, the Father, the Word, and the Holy Ghost: and these three are one." Most Christians would agree with this teaching on the Trinity. The only problem is that there is good evidence that this was not in the original text of 1 John. In fact, it crept into the Latin versions first and was translated back into Greek to give it credibility. When he set out to print a Greek New Testament, Erasmus said he would include the reading if one Greek manuscript could be found that contained it. A very late Greek manuscript that had the reading, obviously translated from the Latin and inserted into the Greek text, was produced. In order to keep his word, Erasmus included it in his text. That is why it is in the text of the KJV.

In the Old Testament certain changes were made by the scribes because the passages had statements in them that appeared to be irreverent toward God. These are called the *tiqqune sopherim* (decrees of the scribes). Instead of the Lord standing yet before Abraham, the reading is changed to Abraham standing before the Lord (Genesis 18:22). Instead of the sons of Eli cursing God, the scribes have the sons of Eli bringing a curse upon themselves (1 Samuel 3:13). Other such changes are thought to be in Job 32:3, where Job's friends condemned Job instead of condemning God. Also it is possible that in Ezekiel 8:17 the original reading was "put the branch to his (God's) nose," and it was changed to "put the branch to their nose." It is not known for sure what is indicated by putting the branch to the nose; perhaps it is some vulgar sign.

The Old Testament was copied by scribes called Masoretes from about A.D. 100 to 500. These scribes were very meticulous in their work. If they found a reading they thought was in error, they would reproduce the error and put what they thought was the correct reading in the margin. The error written in the text was called the *kethibh* (written). The marginal reading, the one intended to be read, was the *qere* (read). The Masoretes were also the ones who put the vowels into the Hebrew text. Originally the Hebrew text was composed of consonants only. In early times certain letters began to stand for vowels, but the Masoretes invented a system of dots and dashes above and below the letters to serve as vowels. Texts with these vowels are called "pointed" texts. Those with only the consonants are called the "unpointed" texts.

The Jews had a curious idea regarding worn-out manuscripts. Instead of preserving them, they would destroy them, usually by burning. Perhaps this was done lest the old manuscripts should be desecrated or irreverently treated. Some early fragments have turned up in genizahs, such as the discovery of the Cairo Genizah by Solomon Schechter in 1890. Genizahs were to the synagogues what the interior of the pulpit stand is in the churches today—a repository of bits and pieces collected over the years.

Until recently there were no extensive Hebrew manuscripts dating before A.D. 1000. Serious questions was raised as to the accuracy of the Hebrew text of the Masoretes (the Masoretic Text, often abbreviated as MT). How could one be sure that the scribes preserved the text through several centuries of transmission? Most of these fears were allayed by the discovery of the Dead Sea Scrolls. In 1946 or 1947 many copies of Old Testament books dating from the time of Christ or before were found in caves near the Dead Sea.

The story of the discovery of the Dead Sea Scrolls is shadowy in some of its details, but generally here is the way it happened. About 1946 an Arab boy was trying to get a goat down from one of the cliffs near the Dead Sea. Not wanting to climb up the cliff, he threw some rocks hoping to scare the goat out. As the rocks landed, he heard a crashing sound, so he went up to investigate. There he found the rocks had hit some old jars that contained some ancient scrolls. Some say the boy took one of the scrolls home and kept it for nearly a year before it came to the public eye. But by 1947 word had leaked out, and some scholars were investigating the caves and uncovering thousands of large scrolls and tiny fragments. Parts of every book of the Old Testament except Esther have been found. Other writings also have been found, such as a *Manual of Discipline,* some psalms, some commentaries on biblical books, a treatise on the war between the sons of light and the sons of darkness, and other interesting works. Certainly the discovery of the Dead Sea Scrolls is one of the outstanding finds of this century.

It is interesting that when verification is needed, the Lord has a way of providing it. When serious questions were raised in the 19th century about the historical reliability of the Scriptures, the science of archaeology arose. And to a large extent archaeology has created a healthy respect for the accuracy of the biblical record. Also, at a time when the text of the Bible was under serious question, the discovery of the Dead Sea Scrolls almost completely dispelled doubt regarding the accuracy of the Masoretic Text.

HISTORY OF THE NEW TESTAMENT TEXT

Papyrus easily rots in damp climates. A few papyrus fragments have been found at Herculaneum and Pompeii, but by far the largest amount of papyrus has been found in Egypt. In this hot, dry climate the papyrus can keep indefinitely. In Egypt papyrus has been found dating several centuries before Christ. If an original New Testament manuscript happened to be buried in the sands of Egypt, it could still be awaiting discovery. However, in a damp climate such as that of Palestine, the papyrus would soon rot.

A. Manuscripts

Early Papyri—The earliest fragment of a New Testament book is the Rylands Papyrus. This is a portion of John 18 dating from around A.D. 125-150. Since the original Gospel of John was written about 90-100, it is possible that this papyrus could be a copy of the original, or perhaps made from a direct copy of the original. Of course, it is so fragmentary that it is not much help in reconstructing the text of the Gospel.

The earliest papyrus of any significant length is the Bodmer Papyrus, also of the Gospel of John. It contains chapters of 1-14 of the Gospel, and dates from about A.D. 200. One interesting feature of this papyrus is its omission of the Pericope of the Adulterous Woman from John 8.

Perhaps the most significant collection of New Testament books from the third century is the Chester Beatty Papyri. These contain parts of 15 books of the New Testament. There are three main manuscripts:

p^{45}, p^{46}, and p^{47}. P^{45} contains most of the four Gospels; p^{46}, letters of Paul; and p^{47}, the book of Revelation. They were named after the man who acquired them in 1930 from Egypt and brought them to London.

Uncials—Even though the papyri are the earliest copies of New Testament books, they are too fragmentary to be of great help in reconstructing the entire text of the New Testament. The greatest help in this would be the uncials. The word *uncial* means "inch high," and refers to the large letters in which they were written. They look much like the printed capital letters, with all of the word run together and little if any punctuation.

Six major uncials have been found, dating from the fourth to the sixth centuries. The most significant of all is Codex Vaticanus. (*Codex* refers to the book form in contrast with the earlier scroll form.) As the name suggests, this manuscript is in the Vatican in Rome. In the fourth century the emperor Constantine commissioned Eusebius to make copies of the Christian scriptures. It is possible that Vaticanus is one of those made at that time. Larger and more complete texts of the New Testament are not found before the fourth century. This is probably because of the efforts of Roman emperors to destroy Christianity, and with it their writings. Only smaller portions of scriptures were kept, such as could be safely hidden from their persecutors. Now with the persecution over, and a Christian emperor on the throne, copies of the Scriptures appeared in abundance. The Vaticanus contains all of the New Testament down through Hebrews; it also has the Greek text of the Old Testament.

The most dramatic story of a manuscript discovery is the one of Codex Sinaiticus. As its name suggests, it was found at Mt. Sinai. The most famous manuscript collector of all time was F. C. Tischendorf. While visiting a monastery on Mt. Sinai in 1844, Tischendorf found 42 leaves of an ancient manuscript in a basket ready to be thrown into the fire. He found upon examination that they were pages from the Septuagint. He asked permission to have them. The abbot gave him the 42 leaves but refused to let him have the rest. In 1853 he returned to Sinai to copy the rest of the manuscript. At first he thought the manuscript had been lost or destroyed. At length the steward showed him an old manuscript wrapped in a cloth. He studied it all night, but was not permitted to take it with him. The Russian Government secured it in 1859, and it was then bought in 1933 by the British Government; presently Sinaiticus is in the British Museum.

A third uncial is the Alexandrinus. It dates from the fifth century and gets its name from Alexandria in Egypt. Cyril Lucar, the patriarch of Alexandria, presented this manuscript to King Charles I of England in 1627.

A fourth uncial is Codex Ephraemi. This is a palimpsest. A palimpsest, literally meaning "rubbed again," is a manuscript that has been written on twice. Someone had tried to erase a text of the Bible and printed over it some writings of a fourth century Syriac father named Ephraem. A great deal of work has been done in an attempt to recover the ancient text that has been rubbed out. This text also dates from the fifth century.

The fifth uncial is Codex Beza. The Genevan Reformer, Theodore Beza, presented this text to the University of Cambridge in 1581. This manuscript is bilingual, written in both Greek and Latin. It has a number of additions in the text that are not found in the other uncials. These variations have become known as Western Readings, because they are prominent in texts from the western part of the Roman world. This manuscript dates from about the sixth century. One of the most famous readings is Acts 8:37, the confession of the Ethiopian eunuch. This is found in a sixth century manuscript, Laudianus.

A sixth uncial is the Washington Codex, containing only the Gospels. C. L. Freer acquired this manuscript for the United States in 1906; consequently it is often referred to as the Freer Gospels. It dates from the fourth or fifth century.

These six unicals are usually referred to by their Code letters. They are as follows:

Vaticanus—B	Ephraemi—C
Sinaiticus—'Aleph (ℵ)	Beza—D
Alexandrinus—A	Washington—W

Minuscules—As the years went by, the scribes began to copy the manuscripts in a more flowing, cursive style of writing instead of the larger printing as in the uncials. These cursive manuscripts were also known as minuscules. The minuscules are far more numerous than the uncials, and also are later and less authoritative. They are referred to by Arabic numerals.

Lectionaries—Lectionaries are portions of scripture that have been copied out for reading in the worship services. Many of these are quite ancient. Of course, the main drawback to these is that they are fragmentary. Often only a few verses, or a chapter at the most, appear.

B. Versions

Aramaic—In ancient times the Scriptures were translated into the languages of other peoples. These translations are known as versions. After the Babylonian exile the Jews began to speak Aramaic. By the time of Christ the Hebrew of the Old Testament was known and spoken only by the rabbis and men of the synagogue. There is good evidence that Jesus spoke Aramaic while he walked on this earth. Mark records some of the Aramaic expressions of Jesus: *Talitha Cumi* (5:41) and *Ephphatha* (7:34). In the intertestamental times Aramaic paraphrases of the Old Testament arose, known as targums. The word *targum* comes from a root meaning "to interpret, translate."

Greek—In the third century B.C. a Greek translation of the Old Testament was produced in Egypt. A spurious document, the *Letter of Aristeas,* tells the supposed history of this translation. Ptolemy Philadelphus of Egypt requested that a copy of the Hebrew Scriptures be translated into Greek for his library in Alexandria. Six elders from each of the 12 tribes worked for 72 days to produce the translation of the Pentateuch. Of course, the details of his account are open to serious doubt. This translation was known as the Septuagint, from the Latin *septuaginta,* which means "70." Often the symbol LXX is used to refer to it. The Septuagint was the Bible of the Greek-speaking Jews in the time of Christ. Many of the Old Testament quotations in the New Testament are from the Septuagint.

Latin—The New Testament, as well as the Old, was translated very early into languages of people where Christianity had gone. In North Africa a number of Old Latin versions arose. Shortly before A.D. 400 Pope Damasus commissioned Jerome to make one authoritative version in Latin for the churches. He wanted it to be put into the vulgar (common) language of the people. This production came to be known as the Vulgate. In the course of time it became the authoritative text for the Roman Catholic Church.

Syriac—Very early the New Testament was also translated into the Syrian tongue. About A.D. 170,

Tatian produced a harmony of the Gospels in the Syriac. It was called the *Diatessaron* ("through the four"). Soon after that, the entire Bible was translated into the Syriac. Some of these are the Peshitta, Harklean, and Philoxenian. *Peshitta* means "simple," the simple language, that everyone could understand. The others were named from the men who took the lead in producing them.

Others—The Scriptures were soon translated into many other languages. In Egypt were the Coptic versions: the Bohairic, Sahidic, etc. There were also Gothic, Georgian, Ethiopic, Arabic and Aramean. Since these translations were made many years earlier than the extant Greek manuscripts, they give evidence of textual readings that are quite helpful. Of course, the originals of these versions have also been lost. So, there is the textual problem with each of them since errors also have crept into their texts as well.

C. Patristic Citations

A third source for reconstructing the text, after the manuscripts and the versions, is the patristic citations, the quotes from the church fathers. Writings of church leaders who lived in the second and third centuries are available. They give testimony of the biblical text as it stood in their days. The writings of Clement of Rome (A.D. 95), Ignatius (110), Irenaeus (180), Justin Martyr (150), and others are a great help in textual criticism.

Besides the antiquity of these citations, there is the added advantage of telling from where certain readings crept into the text. For example, if only the North African fathers give a certain reading, it is certain that the origin of this particular variation must have been in North Africa.

68

There are also some problems. The citations of the fathers are incomplete. They do not always quote the verse the textual critic wishes they did. A complete text cannot be reconstructed from their scattered quotes. They also quote from memory at times, or at least from an imperfect text. Also their original works are not available and so there is the problem of textual criticism regarding their writings.

TEXTUAL CRITICISM

If a scribe has two or more manuscripts, how can he tell which is the more accurate one? With the thousands of manuscripts on hand today, how can one decide which variant reading is the genuine one? Here are some of the basic rules followed in the process of textual criticism.

1. *Take the older reading.* Everything else being equal, the older reading should be the accurate one. It is nearer the original; it has probably been copied fewer times and so has less chance for error.

2. *Take the reading supported by the most ancient witnesses.* Again, everything being equal, the reading that appears in most of the ancient manuscripts stands to be the correct one. This is a case of majority rule.

3. *Reconstruct the history of the variant.* If there are two or three variant readings, and one reading can be seen to be the one from which the others came, chances are that that reading is the original one. Sometimes it is possible to see how a certain variant reading came about, by wrongly dividing a word, by confusing two similar letters, etc.

4. *Prefer quality over quantity of witnesses.* For example, one manuscript from the third century would carry more weight than 10 from the 14th century. Weigh, do not count, the evidence.

5. *Prefer the shorter reading.* Scribes tend to elaborate more than to omit. Seldom will something be left out, but often extraneous material will be added.

6. *Prefer the more difficult reading.* Scribes tend to smooth out difficult passages. They often try to improve the reading, but often complicate the problem. The more difficult reading is most often the older one.[2]

SUMMATION

In the science of lower criticism one stands overwhelmed at the multitude of manuscripts he has to deal with. The problem in textual criticism of the New Testament is not the scarcity of materials to work with, but the sheer abundance of them. For example, Homer's *Iliad* is preserved in 457 papryi, 2 uncials, and 188 minuscules. The works of Euripides is 54 papryi and 276 parchment manuscripts.[3] But there are approximately 5,357 manuscripts of the New Testament in Greek alone. Add to this the evidence of the versions, and there are over 10,000 manuscripts with which to work.

Textual criticism has been refined to such a fine art that today there is serious doubt over less than one in one thousand words in the New Testament. Christians today have a better text than did the Christians of the third century. About the only way one could improve on the present text would be to find the autographs. There is no doctrine of the Bible that is in doubt because of textual uncertainty.

THE PRINTED NEW TESTAMENT

The year 1456 was a very significant year in textual criticism. That was the year of the invention of the printing press. This was the year that Gutenberg printed the now famous Gutenberg Bible. The invention of a press with movable type ushered in the beginning of the printed texts and the close of the handwritten copies of the Bible. Once the type was perfectly set, endless numbers of flawless copies exactly alike could be produced. No longer was there the problem of variations in every manuscript.

The first person who printed the New Testament in Greek was a man from Rotterdam named Erasmus. His first edition appeared in 1516. The second printed Greek text was the work of Cardinal Ximenes from Complutum in Spain. Since Ximenes' edition was done in more than one language and since it was produced in Complutum, it was known as the Complutensian Polyglot. Ximenes and Erasmus were in a race to see which one could be the first to issue a printed Greek New Testament. The pope would not allow Ximenes to issue his Polyglot until he had returned all of his manuscript. Therefore, Erasmus won the race. Ximenes had his work finished in 1514, but it was not published until 1520.

The work of Erasmus was hastily done and had many shortcomings. Often where no Greek text was available, he would translate from the Latin Bible back into the Greek. Erasmus produced several editions of his work. The fourth edition (1527) is the definitive one.

In 1546 a printed edition of the Greek New Testament was produced by Robert Estienne in Paris. He is better known as Stephanus. This edition was based on the work of Erasmus. Stephanus' third edition (1550) was the first to include a critical apparatus. This is where notations are given to show variant textual readings. His fourth edition (1551) is the first to appear with verse divisions. It has been facetiously said that Stephanus was riding on his

71

horse and reading his Bible. Every time the horse jostled him, he marked the end of a verse. Some verses may not be divided in the best manner, but certainly more care than this was exercised in the verse divisions.

Another Greek text was published by Theodore Beza, the leader of the Geneva school after the death of John Calvin. He published nine editions of the Greek text. His text greatly influenced the King James Version.

Two brothers, Bonaventure and Abraham Elzevir, issued a text in 1629. They advertised in the preface to their 1633 edition, "Therefore you have the text now received by all, in which we give nothing changed or corrupted." The Latin for the "text received" is *Textus Receptus*. This term and this type of text became the standard for many years.

About the time the *Textus Receptus* was being widely accepted as *the* text, and the King James Version was gaining in popularity, Codex Alexandrinus came to England. Codex Alexandrinus was much older than the manuscripts used to produce the *Textus Receptus*, and in places it showed marked differences. It was not long until serious doubt was raised concerning the validity of the *Textus Receptus*.

John Mill (1645-1710) collected many ancient manuscripts and cited 30,000 variations from the text of Stephanus. He raised serious doubts as to the reliability of the received text. J. A. Bengel (1687-1752) suggested that texts should be divided into families. For example, those manuscripts that came from Africa all bore marked similarities; the same was true of those from Asia, and those from the western part of the empire. He divided the manuscripts into Asian and African families. J. J. Griesbach (1745-1812) further divided the manuscripts into three families: Alexandrian,

Western and Byzantine.

The first man to issue a Greek text that marked a total break from the *Textus Receptus* was Karl Lachmann (1793-1851). The wealth of ancient manuscripts discovered in the 19th century confirmed suspicion regarding the reliability of the *Textus Receptus*.

Two of the greatest textual critics of recent times were Brooke Foss Westcott and John Anthony Hort. In 1881 they issued their Greek Text, which is close to the one regarded today to be most accurate. They divided the manuscripts into four families: (1) Neutral. These are the purest possible; into this category they placed Vaticanus and Sinaiticus. (2) Alexandrian. These are texts that came from the neutral texts but are later and have more corruptions. (3) Western. These are manuscripts that have been carelessly copied. They have many additions and expansions in the text. (4) Syrian (Byzantine). These comprise the latest and least authoritative manuscripts. The *Textus Receptus* was drawn up from these manuscripts.

The work of Westcott and Hort and others before them cast serious doubt on the reliability of the *Textus Receptus*. Of course, the *Textus Receptus* was not without its defenders. J. W. Burgon, Edward Miller and F. H. A. Scrivener spoke out long and loud in its defense. They argued that God would not let an obscure text exist for so long. They also pointed out that the majority of extant manuscripts (although they were much later manuscripts) favored the *Textus Receptus*.

The Nestle text, by Eberhard and his son Erwin Nestle, became the most widely accepted text in the early part of the 20th century. It, along with the Bible Societies' text, is the one most often used today. The Bible Societies' text is a production that is the result of a united effort of men such as Kurt Aland, Matthew Black, Bruce Metzger, Allen Wikgren and others who have combined their scholarship to produce a text that is as near to the original as is humanly possible to do today. The percentage of error in today's Greek text is less than one tenth of one percent.

The study of textual criticism is a great faith builder. Even though the text was written down by man, copied by man and printed by man—and even though uncertainties can be found—they are so minimal that they hardly deserve serious considerations by the average Bible student. If you have been staying awake worrying whether or not you have the words of the apostles as they wrote them down, sleep well tonight. You can trust your Bible!

FOOTNOTES

[1]Bruce M. Metzger, *The Text of the New Testament* (New York: Oxford University Press, 1968), p. 17.

[2]Ira M. Price, *The Ancestry of our English Bible,* Third revised edition by William A. Irwin and Allen P. Wikgren (New York: Harper & Row, 1956, p. 221.

[3]Metzger, p. 34.

CHAPTER IV
Are the Translations Reliable?

One gentleman was heard to say, "There's no use in learning Greek. If the Lord had wanted us to know Greek, he would have had the Bible written in that language in the first place." Well, that is just what he did, in the New Testament.

Most people realize that the Bible was not originally written in English. The apostles did not use the King James Version. In fact, the Bible was originally written in three different languages. Most of the Old Testament was written in Hebrew. A small portion (Jeremiah 10:11; Daniel 2:4-7:28; Ezra 4:8-6:18; 7:12-26) was written in Aramaic. The New Testament was written in Greek.

THE ORIGINAL LANGUAGES OF THE BIBLE

Hebrew. There is evidences from the earliest Hebrew inscriptions that a Phoenician type script was used during the time the Old Testament was being written. About the time of Ezra this was replaced with the square Assyrian characters. Most of the extant manuscripts have the square characters.

One interesting feature about Hebrew is that it reads "backwards," that is, from right to left. The front of a Hebrew Bible is on the back, and as one reads, he progresses from the back to the front. Of course, the Hebrews would say that those who speak English are the ones who read backwards.

Another feature of Hebrew is that originally the language consisted of only consonants. One would mentally add the vowels as he would read. It was not until the first few centuries after Christ that vowels were added to the Hebrew text. This peculiarity caused some problems in pronunciation. For example, the personal name for God in the Old Testament, YHWH, was considered so holy that it was not to be pronounced. Since in early times there were no vowels indicated to assist in pronunciation, and there are no recordings of how the name was spoken, no one today knows how it is to be pronounced. When the Hebrews read YHWH, they substituted another word in its place, a word meaning "lord," *adonay*. The word *Jehovah* is a combination of the vowels for *adonay* and the consonants for the divine name, YHWH or JHVH.

Aramaic. Aramaic became the universal language of the Fertile Crescent about the time of the Babylonian exile. The Jews who returned from exile spoke Aramaic. When the people returned home, they stood as the law was read to them. But while the reading was given in Hebrew, there were some appointed to translate it into Aramaic so the people could understand (Nehemiah 8:8).

Aramaic was an ancient language. There is evidence that it was spoken as early as the days of the patriarchs. In Genesis 31:47 Jacob and Laban had set up a pile of stones and agreed to stay on opposite sides of it. Jacob called it *Galeed* (Hebrew for heap of witness); Laban called it *Jegarsahadutha* (Aramaic for heap of witness).

In New Testament days the people of Palestine spoke Aramaic. Jesus' language around his home was Aramaic. He spoke Aramaic when he performed some miracles.

76

He raised Jairus' daughter with the Aramaic, *"Talitha cumi"* (Mark 5:41). He healed the deaf mute with the Aramaic, *"Ephphatha"* (Mark 7:34). His cry on the cross *(Eloi, Eloi lama sabachthani)* is a mixture of Hebrew and Aramaic. The word he used to address his father, *Abba,* is the Aramaic word that children used to call their fathers. Other Aramaic expressions in the New Testament are *Corban* (Mark 7:11), *Akeldama* (Acts 1:19), and the little prayer in 1 Corinthians 16:22, *Maranatha* (O Lord come).

Greek. The Greek of the New Testament is known as *Koine. Koine* means the common, everyday language as contrasted with the older classical Greek. Adolph Deissmann has done a great service in pointing out from the study of non-literary papyri that the New Testament was written in the everyday language of the people.[1]

The New Testament uses words taken from every walk of life. Particularly interesting are some terms used in the commercial world. For example, in Matthew 6 Jesus warned against doing righteousness in order to be seen of men. Twice he said that those who did such had already received their reward (verses 2 and 5). The Greek word here is a commercial term *(apecho)* meaning "paid in full." When a person had made the last payment and was out of debt, the merchant would write on his bill *apecho* (paid in full). Jesus says that those who do their righteousness to be seen of men have been paid in full. They should not expect any further reward from the heavenly Father.

Three times Paul speaks of the Holy Spirit as the *"earnest* of our inheritance" (2 Corinthians 1:22; 5:5; Ephesians 1:14). This Greek word for "earnest," *arrabon,* literally means "down payment." The idea is that God has given to Christians the Holy Spirit now.

77

That is a down payment, a pledge that later he will give the rest of what he has promised. One makes a down payment as a pledge that he will pay the rest of the debt in time. There is certainty in the promises of God. He has given a down payment already—his Spirit in the hearts of his children.

It has been said, "The Greeks have a word for it." Perhaps there is no other language more versatile and yet precise than the *Koine* Greek. It is worthy of note that God chose this beautiful, exact and versatile language in which to clothe the message of salvation. As one studies Greek, he is continually impressed with the preciseness in the tenses, the breadth of expression permitted by the large vocabulary, and the general excellence of this language. What better choice could have been made for a language in which to tell of redemption?

Of course, everyone cannot be skilled in the reading of Hebrew, Greek and Aramaic. Therefore, he will have to depend on the scholarship of others for what the Bible actually says. This raises a question of how much can those who know only English depend on the translation of others? Can one trust the English Bible? How can he be certain that the meaning has not been changed in places? Are there translations that are unsafe? What are the best translations?

Certainly if one wishes to be a scholar in biblical studies, he needs to know the original languages of the Bible. One has said that studying the Bible through a translation is like washing one's feet with your socks on. Even more emphatic is the statement that it is like kissing one's girlfriend through a handkerchief. Nothing can take the place of knowing firsthand the languages of the Bible.

But on the other hand, there is no real cause for

worry among those who do not know the original languages. The Bible has been translated into English quite accurately. Although some versions (translations) are better than others, there is no translation which has distorted the truth so badly that one cannot find the way of salvation by reading it. It is often best to use the same version as the person one is trying to teach.

Many seem to have the idea that if they knew the original languages there would be hidden truths open to him that were never expressed in their English versions. This is not usually the case. Very often people ask, "What does the Greek say on that?" Usually the best answer is, "The same thing the English says." The next best thing to knowing the original languages is to use several different English versions. All of the shades of meanings can be seen, and it is easy to tell which version is in error in a particular translation.

Quite often one of the best advantages in knowing Greek is in being able to answer ridiculous arguments that others have made from the Greek. It is easy to tell the average audience, "The Greek says this." No one in the audience knows Greek, and so the argument is ended. Marshall Keeble was asked once after he had finished preaching, "Brother Keeble, what does the Greek say on this?" He didn't know any Greek, and so he asked the audience, "How many of you know Greek?" No one raised his hand. So brother Keeble replied, "It wouldn't do any good to tell you, since no one here knows Greek." Jack McKinney, while serving as missionary in Switzerland, heard a visiting American evangelist asked the same question, "What does the Greek say on this?" The evangelist remembered how brother Keebler got out of the embarrassing situation, and since he didn't know Greek either, he asked the audience, "How many of you know Greek?" To his surprise about 12 hands went up!

THE PERILS OF A TRANSLATOR

One of the biggest problems in translating the Scriptures is the desire to be accurate and at the same time readable. A very literal translation of the Scriptures would be hardly understandable. The infinitive and participial constructions in Greek are not idiomatic in English. If one takes the liberty to make a smooth idiomatic translation in English, he ceases to be literal. The smoother the translation, quite often, the more one's own opinions and interpretations intrude into the translation. The more literal the translation, the less readable, and often the less understandable is the translation. The ideal translation is one that remains true to the original reading, being just as explicit and ambiguous as the original, and at the same time one that is readable.

As mentioned earlier, the New Testament was written in the everyday language of the people. The Scriptures appeared to them in an exalted conversational style, much like the newspaper reads. It did not come to them in archaic, stilted, often unknown expressions or style. The use of "thee," "thou," "wast" and "hath" is not holy language. This was the way people in 17th century England spoke, The influence of the King James Version (published in 1611) has led many to regard such manner of expressions as holy language. This language is no more holy language than Shakespeare's or that of any other literature from that time.

Help from Archaelogy. While a multitude of manuscripts have been discovered in the past two centuries and helped greatly in reconstructing the original text, other discoveries have aided in producing more accurate translations of the Scriptures. Place names have been identified, unclear expressions have been brought to light, and many general improvements in the art of translations have occurred in the past century.

In 1 Samuel 13:21 the King James Version reads, "Yet they had a file for their mattocks." The word translated "file" is the Hebrew *pim*; in 1611 no one knew the meaning of this Hebrew word. Recently small stones having *pim* written on them have been found in Palestine. It is now thought that a *pim* was a weight of money, probably a small weight of silver. This information is seen in the Revised Standard Version's reading of the verse, "and the charge was a pim for the plowshares and for the mattocks." The verse is telling about the monopoly that the Philistines had on iron. They would not permit the Israelites to have any iron weapons, but they did allow them to have iron agricultural tools. They charged the Israelites for maintenance of their farming implements.

Another illustration is seen in 2 Kings 23:29. Here the King James Version reads, "In his days Pharaoh-nechoh king of Egypt went up against the king of Assyria to the river Euphrates." This sounds as if the king of Egypt and the king of Assyria were fighting each other. The discovery of the Babylonian Chronicle has made it clear that these two kings were not enemies, but they fought together against a common foe, Nebuchadnezzar, king of Babylon. This necessitated a change in the way a particular Hebrew word (*'al*) was translated. The Hebrew word could mean "against"; it could also be translated "to." This change is seen in later translations such as the New American Standard Version, "In his days Pharaoh Neco king of Egypt went up to the king of Assyria." It is now known that

Nebuchadnezzar defeated the combined forces of Egypt and Assyria at Carchemish in 605 B.C. This made him the undisputed ruler of the Fertile Crescent and forever ended the Assyrian threat.

These are just two illustrations of the help that archaeology has been to translators. There are still some passages that are difficult to translate. Possibly a few erroneous translations are still present in modern English versions which later discoveries will correct. But these problems are not of great consequence. The message of salvation and basic Christian doctrines are in no way affected by these uncertainties in translations. It is good to know that a *pim* is a weight of money instead of a file. It is also good to learn that the kings of Egypt and Assyria were fighting on the same side, but these minutiae do not affect the message of salvation.

A BRIEF HISTORY OF ENGLISH TRANSLATIONS

The earliest known attempt to put the Bible into English is the Lindesfarne Gospels, dating from around A.D. 700. This is a Latin text of the Gospels with an Anglo-Saxon interlinear penned in by some scribe.

Other portions of the Scriptures were put into English as more English speaking people were converted to Christianity. But the first man to translate the entire Bible into English was John Wycliffe. This work was completed around 1382; Wycliffe died in 1384. Much of his work was done while he was in prison.

The first man to print the New Testament into English was William Tyndale (1526). He is regarded by many as the Father of the English Bible. The church authorities in England disapproved putting the Bible into the language of the masses and so Tyndale had to leave the country. His work was done at Cologne, Worms and Marburg. Later he moved to Antwerp. He smuggled his copies of the New Testament back into England. These early translations were quite imperfect. Sir Thomas More said, "To study to find errors in Tyndale's book was like studying to find water in the sea."[2] Tyndale died a martyr's death.

Even before his death, Tyndale's Bible was used by most of the churches in England. His work was continued by Miles Coverdale, who is the first to print the entire Bible into English (1535). This was also the first Bible in English to circulate without opposition from the authorities.

In rapid succession several English versions appeared: Matthew's Bible in 1537, and Richard Taverner's Bible and the "Great Bible" in 1539. These were mainly revisions of the work done by Tyndale and Coverdale.

Matthew's Bible was really a completion of Tyndale's work. Tyndale had translated and printed only the New Testament and the Pentateuch and Jonah of the Old Testament. It is mainly the work of John Rogers, a disciple of Tyndale. The name "Matthew's Bible" comes from the name that appears at the foot of the dedication, "Thomas Matthew." Some think this is Rogers himself; others suggest it is the name of one of Rogers' assistants.

Richard Taverner, an Oxford scholar, undertook a complete revision of Matthew's Bible. Since he was a better Greek scholar than he was Hebrew, the translation of the New Testament is of better quality than his translation of the Old Testament. When the Great Bible was produced, the Taverner's Bible quickly fell into disuse.

The Great Bible, so called because of its size, marks the beginning of the great love that English people have had for their Bibles. The printing of the Great Bible began in France, but it was finished in London. It was often used as the pulpit Bible, and was frequently chained to the pulpit, not to keep the people from reading it, but to keep it from being stolen.

Many Protestants fled from England when Mary ascended to the throne. A large settlement of these refugees was found in Geneva, Switzerland. It was here that they produced their version, the Geneva Bible. Because of the strong Calvinistic influence in Switzerland, these refugees became Calvinistic in their thinking, and these influences are seen in their Bible. This work, published in 1560, is the first English Bible to set off verses into separate paragraphs and to put in italics words that are not in the original language but were inserted to make the sense clear. The Geneva Bible is the Bible of Shakespeare. It is also called the "breeches Bible" because of its reading in Genesis 3:7 that Adam and Eve "sewed figge tree leaves together, and made themselves breeches."

The Geneva Bible, next to the work of Tyndale, exerted the greatest influence upon the translators of the King James Version. It was an excellent work. Its accuracy, clarity and beauty of expression soon made it the most popular Bible in English. While the Great Bible was the Bible of the church, the Geneva Bible was the Bible of the people.

Since the Geneva Bible was the Bible of a very small segment of the English speaking Christians and often reflected the Calvinistic thinking of this small segment, it could not be the official Bible for England. Therefore, an attempt was made to produce an official Bible that the masses would accept instead of the Geneva Bible. This work is known as the Bishops' Bible, published in 1568. Although it was the one for the official use in the churches, the masses of the people preferred the

Geneva Bible. In the 43 years between the publishing of the Bishops' Bible and the appearance of the King James Version (1568-1611) 20 editions of the Bishops' Bible came from the press, but nearly 120 editions of the Geneva Bible.

Since there was an abundance of English versions available among the Protestants, there was pressure from the Roman Catholics to produce for their people a Bible in English. If the English speaking Catholics were going to read a Bible in their native tongue instead of Latin, the Roman Church wanted it to be one that had their approval. This led to the publishing of the Rheims-Douai Version. The New Testament was completed in 1582, and the Old Testament in 1609. This translation was made from the Latin Vulgate, not the original Hebrew and Greek. This was done because the Catholic Church held that Jerome's Vulgate was the authoritative Bible of the Church. Of course, this translation of a translation was not of the quality of a translation from the original. In some places the reading is awkward, stiff and even unintelligible. This version was never greatly popular.

For example, in Psalms 57:10 the following reading appears: "Before your thorns did understand the old briar; as living so in wrath he swalloweth them."[3]

The King James Version. Since the failure of the Bishops' Bible to supersede the Geneva Bible, there was a further attempt to produce a Bible that would be the authorized English version. This effort was begun in 1607. Around 50 scholars were engaged in the project, and it was the result of two years and nine months labor. This version first issued from the press in 1611. It was known as the King James Version in honor of the king of England, James. It also became known as the Authorized Version.

It was an excellent work in many ways. Kenyon lists three causes of its superiority:

1. Greek and Hebrew scholarship had greatly increased during the 40 years before 1611.
2. The version was the work of no single man or school.
3. The past 40 years saw an extraordinary growth in English literature. The King James Version reflected this literary excellence.[4]

Like all new versions, it was not readily accepted. People always seem hesitant to forsake the old for the new. Hugh Broughton said that he "had rather be rent in pieces with wild horses, than any such translation by my consent should be urged upon poor churches!" His criticism could be partly due to the fact that he was not asked to serve on the panel of translators.[5] But by the middle of the 17th century it gained undisputed place as the foremost of the English versions. The last edition of the Geneva Bible was in 1644. Slowly but surely the King James Versions became the standard Bible for the English speaking Christians.

Even today the King James Version is the most popular English translation of the Bible. It has undergone many revisions of spelling, punctuation, etc., since its first appearance, but the translation is basically the one made in 1611. The archaic pronouns—thee, thou, thy—still persist. Archaic verb forms—wast, doth, hath—are still there. Most people in the 20th century are reading a Bible written in Elizabethan English from the 17th century.

While it must be admitted that the King James Version is an excellent translation, it should also be pointed out that it is not above error. Translations are made by men, and men are fallible. There is no perfect translation, just as there are no perfect translators.

One interesting example of bias is in 1 Samuel 10:24. When Saul was presented to the people as their new king, they all shouted, "God save the king." The Hebrew literally says, "Let the king live." The familiar cry "God save the king" gives the general sense, but it is not a fair translation.

In Matthew 23:24, resulting from an uncorrected printer's error, the King James Version has Jesus saying, "Ye blind guides, which strain at a gnat, and swallow a camel." This leaves the impression that the people choke trying to swallow a gnat. The Greek should be translated, "which strain *out* a gnat." The Pharisees were so careful about avoiding unclean food that they would strain their wine lest a gnat (an unclean animal) should have fallen into it and they would drink it in the wine. On the other hand they would eat a whole camel (also an unclean animal).

In Acts 12:4 the King James Version says that Herod put Peter into prison intending to bring him forth to the people after Easter. The word translated "Easter" means Passover. There was no Easter in the days of Herod. If there had been, this non-Christian ruler would have not paid any attention to it. Later translations correct this mistake by reading *Passover* instead of *Easter.*

Besides obvious errors such as these, there are also expressions in the King James Version that have changed their meaning or today are quite meaningless. In 1 Corinthians 13 Paul speaks of the greatest gift of all, charity. In 1611 *charity* was a synonym for *love.* Today *charity* refers to helping the poor. Paul is not talking about handouts to the poor in 1 Corinthians 13. This should be rendered *love,* not *charity.*

In 1 Thessalonians 4:15 the King James Version has

Paul saying that we who are alive at Christ's coming will not "prevent them which are asleep." In 1611 "prevent" meant to precede; today it means to hinder. Later translations read *precede* where the King James Version has *prevent*.

In 2 Timothy 4:1 the King James Version says that God will judge the quick and the dead. The work *quick* meant "alive" in 1611. Such a use is still seen in the "quick" of a fingernail; that is the part that is alive. It would be more meaningful to render the passage as the living and the dead. The same is true in Hebrews 4:12, where it is said that the word of God is quick and powerful; the meaning is alive and powerful.

As was shown in the earlier chapter, the King James Version was translated from a decidedly inferior Greek text as compared with the ones available today. None of the six major manuscripts were used in the production of the King James Version. Textual criticism had hardly come into its own by 1611. A translation can be no better than the text used. Several questionable readings appear in the King James Version, such as 1 John 5:7 and Acts 8:37.

Some of the readings in the King James Version appear a bit crude because of a change in word meanings and literary taste. In Jeremiah 4:19 the King James Version has Jeremiah cry, "My bowels! My bowels!" Later versions read, "My anguish! My anguish!" In early times people thought the bowels were the seat of one's emotions. Jeremiah is not complaining of a physical ailment; he is expressing grief over the plight of his people. Compare the reading of the King James Version in Philippians 2:1, "if any bowels and mercies." "Tender compassion" would make a much better reading than "bowels."

These criticisms are not intended to leave the impression that the King James Version should not be used, or that it is unreliable. They are given to show that even the "sacred cow" of some people as regarding versions is susceptible to error. There is no perfect translation. The King James Version is far from perfect. In fact, there is evidence that today there are versions that in many ways are superior to the King James Version. Yet the problems with the King James Version are not so great as to alter the message of the Bible. The message of salvation and God's plan for man are clearly seen in this great translation of three centuries ago. You can trust the message in this translation.

Later English Versions. The King James Version went virtually unchallenged for over 200 years. The first serious attempt to improve upon the King James Version was the English Revised Version of 1881. The discovery of many ancient manuscripts plus the critical work of men such as Westcott and Hort caused serious doubts about the text from which the King James Version was translated.

Without question the English Revised Version is based upon a better Greek text than is the King James Version. Although many word changes were made (*love* for *charity; Sheol* and *Hades* for *hell*), it is generally not much more readable than is the King James Version. It has not replaced the King James Version, nor has it ever enjoyed the popularity of it.

An American edition of the 1881 English Revised Version appeared in 1901, known as the American Standard Version. It is basically the same as the 1881 edition, except it was made more readable to the American people. A new paragraph system was introduced. Instead of the separate verses being set off as paragraphs, a series of verses on the same topic were grouped into a single paragraph. It also introduced the name *Jehovah* for *Lord*. Perhaps the American Standard Version comes nearest to being a literal translation of the Greek, but it is not the most readable. Neither is it as melodious and in many respects in as high a literary style as is the King James Version. It has not replaced the King James Version in popularity; in fact, today it is being replaced by later works, such as the New American Standard Version.

The pronouncement of Deissmann that the New Testament was written in the everyday language of the people gave an impetus to the rise of modern speech translations. Why not put the Bible into the everyday language of the people? Over 20 modern speech translations have appeared in the 20th century. Among them are those by Weymouth (1903), Moffatt (1913, 1924), Goodspeed (1923) and Phillips (1958). The modern speech versions seek to give the thought of the original in conversational English. They do not pretend to be a word-for-word translation. Of course, such freedom in translation opens the door for error and also involves more opinion and interpretation of the translator. Many people are reluctant to receive them because they do not "sound like" the Bible. F. F. Bruce tells of a woman whose minister read to her a portion of Moffatt's translation. She said, "Yes, that was very nice, but won't you read a bit of the Word of God before you go?"[6]

The Revised Standard Version (1946 for the New Testament; 1952 for the complete Bible) was a significant contribution to the long line of English translations. It was an attempt to preserve the accuracy of the earlier standard versions yet to make it more readable to the general public. It included the benefits of the past century of scholarship. As was shown earlier, it incorporated the light shed from archaeology, as in the translations of *pim* in 1 Samuel 13:21. It also was produced by men who had access to the best possible Greek and Hebrew texts of the day.

More conservative Christians criticized the Revised Standard Version for not being as literal as the King James or American Standard. Particularly it was asserted that the rendering of Isaiah 7:14 and John 3:16 smacked of liberalism.

Isaiah 7:14 in the Revised Standard Version has "young woman" in the place of "virgin" in the prophecy of the virgin birth; "a young woman will conceive and bear a son." The Hebrew word is *almah,* not *bethulah,* which is the usual word for *virgin.* The Revised Standard Version certainly does not deny the virgin birth of Jesus, because in Matthew 1:23 it plainly reads virgin in the quotation from Isaiah 7:14. The translation "young woman" in Isaiah 7:14 has much to commend it. There is good evidence that this passage is a double prophecy, one with two applications. Ahaz, king of Judah, was threatened by a coalition of Ephraim and Syria. Isaiah told him that he had no need to fear these two kingdoms. Before a young woman could conceive and bear a child, and that child get old enough to know good from evil, those two kings and their kingdoms would be gone. This word of encouragement was spoken about 735 B.C. Syria was destroyed in 732; Ephraim was destroyed in 722. It would take about 13 years for a woman to conceive, bear a child and for that child to get old enough to know good from evil. But this passage had a second meaning, a reference to the virgin birth of the Christ. Therefore, Isaiah used a word

91

for *woman (almah)* which could mean a virgin or just a young woman. The Greek word for *virgin* in Matthew 1:23 *(parthenos)* demands the translation "virgin," which the Revised Standard Version gives.

In John 3:16 the Revised Standard Version says that God gave his "only son," instead of "only begotten son." This is taken by some as a blow at the divinity of Jesus. The word translated "only" (or "only begotten") is *monogenes*, which literally means "one of a kind." It does not necessarily denote the only child. Isaac is called Abraham's only begotten (Hebrews 11:17); yet Abraham had other children. Even the King James Version is not consistent in its translation of *monogenes*. In Luke 7:12 the young man whom Jesus raised from the dead was called "the only son of his mother." The word for *only* is *monogenes*. Why did they not read "only begotten" in this passage?

The Revised Standard Version has been unjustly maligned as an instrument of the devil because of tendencies to liberalism. It is true that the Revised Standard Version has its faults. Remember—no translation is perfect, because no translators are perfect. There is no serious problem with the Revised Standard Version. One would not reject the divinity of Christ because of the way those two passages were translated. As in the case of all other translations, the problems are small; the message of salvation is abundantly clear. You *can* trust your Bible.

The New English Bible is a quality work. The freer rendering of the Greek makes it less literal than the American Standard or the King James or even the Revised Standard Version. But the Greek student can see in the New Testament, especially in the book of Hebrews, many delicate shades of meaning from the

Greek which have been included in the English rendering.

One drawback with the New English Bible is the attempt to give references to time in modern day manner. For example, instead of reading the third hour as does the Greek, the New English Bible would say nine o'clock. This problem is more acute in Acts 20:7, where it says that the disciples met together on Saturday night to break bread. The Jewish day began at sundown. So Saturday night was really Sunday. The New English reading leaves the impression that the disciples broke bread on Saturday instead of the first day of the week.

Another criticism is the rendering of Matthew 16:18, "Thou art Peter, the Rock." There is no justification whatever for including "the Rock." Could this have been done to please the Papists, who maintain that Peter was the rock upon which the church was built?

Another unfortunate reading is in 1 Corinthians 14, where "language of ecstasy" is given for "tongue." The Greek word *glossa* denotes a "tongue," a "language," not necessarily ecstatic utterance.

The *New American Standard Version* is one of the most trustworthy and usable of the recent translations In the preface the Lockman Foundation, producers of the version, listed their fourfold aim:

1. These publications shall be true to the original Hebrew and Greek.
2. They shall be grammatically correct.
3. They shall be understandable to the masses.
4. They shall give the Lord Jesus Christ His proper place, the place which the Word gives Him; no work will ever be personalized.

To a remarkable degree, the translators have accomplished their goal.

SUMMATION

"Why don't they leave the Bible alone and quit trying to change it?" This complaint is heard as some honest, but uninformed people look at the rash of new translations of the Bible which have flooded the market. In recent times there have appeared the New English Bible, New American Standard Version, Good News for Modern Man, the New International Version and many others. People are not trying to change the Bible. These are just efforts of many people to convey the message of salvation in the most intelligible manner they know. Each of these is a translation with strengths and weaknesses, some better than others, some worse. Not one of them is so perverted that one misses the message of the Scriptures. Why not focus on the similarities between the versions instead of the minute differences? They all agree 98% with each other. This should give assurance that one can trust the translations. Compare them. It is easy to see where one is incorrect. By studying a number of translations, it is possible to gain the fine shades of meaning and all the facets of the original.

FOOTNOTES

[1]Adolph Deissmann, *Light from the Ancient East,* translated by L. R. M. Strachan, new and completely revised (New York: George H. Doran Co., 1927).

[2]Cited in F. F. Bruce, *The Books and the Parchments,* revised (Westwood, New Jersey: Fleming H. Revell Company, 1963), p. 223.

[3]Frederic G. Kenyon, *Our Bible and the Ancient Manuscripts,* revised H. W. Adams (New York: Harper & Brothers, 1958), p. 302.

[4]*Ibid.,* p. 206.

[5]Bruce, p. 229.

[6]*Ibid.,* p. 235.

EPILOGUE
Which Is the Best Bible?

People often ask me, "Just which is the best Bible?" My usual answer is, "The best for what?" It all depends on what you want. If you want a dependable translation which is most popular, the King James Version is the best. If you want the most accurate word for word translation, the American Standard Version is as good as any. If you want a more readable version with a high degree of accuracy, the Revised Standard Version would be the one. If you want a freer rendering that does a good job of giving the finer shades of meaning in the original, the New English Bible is good. Personally I use the New American Standard Version in my teaching. It is faithful to the text and is understandable by most people.

Whatever version you use, you can thank hundreds of scholars for their untiring work in textual criticism, grammatical study and related fields for bringing to you a version you can depend on. You *can* trust your Bible!

The Church of Christ
Tuscumbia, Alabama